Navigating Life's Decisions and their Eternal Consequences

Bria Cox

Navigating Life's Decisions and their Eternal Consequences

Bria Cox

Inscript

Bladensburg, Maryland

Contents

Foreword

Greetings to all readers. We are now living in the last and evil days, according to the Bible. This book is organized by topics relevant to today's issues and concerns. It is for Christians walking with God or anyone who is interested in the Word of God broken down and made plain. The Bible is for those who want instructions on how to live on this earth. I hope someone walks away from reading this book with a more in-depth knowledge of who our great God is. This book is the perspective of a millennial woman who has had her fair share of ups and downs in her relationship with God. I would also like to note that when "god" is lowercase, it refers to the enemy, Satan. God the creator is always uppercase. God bless to all my readers.

Introduction

How did we get here? I thought you would never ask. In the beginning (Genesis 1-3), there was a formless void, and God created light. He created the heavens, the earth, and the universe. On separate days, he created plants, animals, and eventually, a man named Adam.

After Adam named the animals, God decided it was not good for man to be alone, so he put Adam to sleep and took one of his ribs. From that rib came the first woman. She was made from man, and she was named Eve.

God told them to be fruitful and multiply. They were allowed to eat from every tree except from the Tree of Knowledge. God commanded them not to eat from that tree because if they did, they would truly die. Then, the serpent slithered in and convinced Eve to eat the fruit from the forbidden tree. He lied and told her she would not die if she ate from it. He told her that her eyes would be opened and she would be like God. Eve disobeyed God and ate the fruit. She convinced Adam to eat the fruit as well.

They had been naked this entire time, but after eating the fruit, they were ashamed, so they made clothes from fig leaves. They were afraid, so they hid themselves. God was walking in the garden and asked them why they were hiding. Adam and Eve confessed to their rebellion and blamed the serpent for the deception. So, God punished all of them. Adam would work and toil for the rest of his life. Eve would have pain during childbirth, and her husband would rule over her. They were going to live forever, but now that sin had entered the world, Adam and Eve would die. As for the serpent, aka Satan, Eve's offspring (Jesus) would crush his head and strike his heel.

Throughout the Old Testament, there are many examples of how God deals with those who are obedient to him versus those who are disobedient. To those who fear God and keep his commandments, they are called the children of God. When his children sinned according to the law, they needed to atone by giving animal sacrifices. But the sacrifices didn't take away the guilty conscience from committing sin.

Fast forward to the New Testament. God sends his only Son to Earth in human form to pay for our sins once and for all. Because Jesus was the Word wrapped in flesh with the Spirit of God, he was a worthy sacrifice. Through the old Adam came death to all, but through the new Adam, Jesus Christ, came life for all who have faith in him. The gift is greater than the trespass. Animal sacrifices are no longer needed. We only need to confess with our mouths that Jesus Christ is Lord and believe he died for our sins and was resurrected. With confession and faith, we are now saved. God made it simple.

Once Jesus was resurrected, he went to the Father in heaven. That was the beginning of the end. Now, he is on his way back. This is called the second coming. Based on the signs of the end times in scripture, we are in the endgame now. One must be ready so that when Jesus returns to rapture the church, they will be gathered in the air with the Savior and spared from the tribulation. To be prepared for his return, the following topics will be helpful for your spiritual journey. The decisions you make in this life will alter your eternal destination. "Therefore, to him who knoweth to do good, but doeth it not, then to him it is a sin" (James 4:17 ASV). It's one thing to be ignorant of the truth, but once you receive knowledge, you will be held accountable for your decisions.

A Void Only He Can Fill

"Come to me, all you who are weary and burdened and I will give you rest. Take my yoke upon you and learn from me, for I am gentle and humble in heart, and you will find rest for your souls" (Matthew 11:28-29).

These two verses are very comforting because they are an invitation to salvation. No matter our gender, race, ethnic group, or age, we all have something in common: we need Jesus. We were created for worship, and there is a void in our souls that only a relationship with God can fill. Nothing else can satisfy that void, not money, material possessions, human beings, etc. All humans face struggles and trials, but when you have Jesus, he gives you the victory. He gives rest to the tired. His yoke is easy, and his burden is light (v. 30). He has a gentle spirit that forgives sins. He is slow to anger but quick to forgive.

There is a solution to every problem on this earth, and the answer is Jesus. Come to him as you are. You don't need fancy clothes. You don't need riches. You don't need a great reputation. Come to him as the born sinner you are, and his blood will make you clean. You will be a new creation. Then, once in Christ, as believers, we are to be one in Spirit and of one mind (Philippians 2:2). We are then co-heirs with Christ. We are to be like-minded, sharing his love, gentleness, and compassion with others. We look out for the interests of others, not focusing on promoting ourselves. As children of God, we put others above ourselves (v3).

Being Content

"I have learned the secret of being content in any and every situation, whether well fed or hungry, whether living in plenty or in want" (Letter of Paul the Apostle to the Philippians 4:12).

We need to take Paul's approach to being content in all circumstances. He wrote this letter to the church in Philippi while he was in prison. Mind you, he had committed no crime and was innocent. He was imprisoned for spreading the good news of Christ. How many of us would be mad and upset if we were imprisoned, even if we were guilty? We probably wouldn't be in good spirits like Paul was. While he was in prison, he encouraged the Saints in Philippi to be content. He lovingly prayed that they abound in love and gain more knowledge. He used his circumstance to proclaim that his imprisonment advanced the gospel.

At the end of the day, it's about preaching the gospel and giving thanks to God. In all situations, be content. The prayers of the righteous will intercede for you as well. Meanwhile, look out for the interests of others, putting your own last. "I am not saying this because I am in need, for I have learned to be content whatever the circumstance" (Philippians 4:11).

We've all had moments when we were in need; maybe we were low on funds or had nothing to eat. Maybe we've also had times where we had plenty and had no reason to worry about anything. God wants us to give thanks in all circumstances and be content in life, no matter how much is in your bank account, what kind of job you have, or whether you are single, married, or divorced. The secret to being content in life, no matter what, is to put your faith in Jesus.

Paul says we can do all things through Christ, which strengthens us (v.13). If we can't be grateful for the things we have now, we will never be ready for God's blessings. If we complain constantly about what's going on right now, then if we are blessed with our desires, we will be even more ungrateful. If we can't learn to be content with what we have, then no matter what we get, we will always want more, and it will never be enough. We need to be at a place in our lives where Jesus is enough. He is sufficient for us. If you never get that house, car, boat, expensive wardrobe, corporate job, wife, husband, or kids, will you be satisfied with Jesus?

Breaking Strongholds

"It is written: Man shall not live on bread alone, but on every word that comes from the mouth of God" (Matthew 4:4).

Psalms 9:9 defines a stronghold as a refuge. A spiritual stronghold refers to any pretension, argument, or knowledge that is against God. The spirit is contrary to the flesh. The enemy blinds the minds of unbelievers.

To demolish spiritual strongholds, we must study the Word daily. One must keep the Word, which is our sword, in our hearts so we are ready for battle. We must study how Jesus fought the adversary. Satan came to him when Jesus was weak from fasting and tried to tempt him. Even so, Jesus kept answering back with God's Word.

Satan also tempts us during vulnerable moments. It is paramount to keep some "it is written" weapons in our artillery chest. Next time you encounter the tempter, tell him, "Away from me, Satan"; use the Word of God against him. We do not fight with the weapons of the world. Our weapons are spiritual and have the divine power to demolish strongholds, arguments, and pretensions that set themselves up against the knowledge of God. We have immense power through Christ, who strengthens us. Jesus understands our struggles. Nothing we go through could compare to what they did to Jesus. He stood up against the adversary and never sinned. Jesus endured more than we could ever even imagine, yet he stood strong. "The Word of God is sharper than any double-edged sword, penetrating even to dividing soul and spirit, joints and marrow; It judges the thoughts and attitudes of the heart" (Hebrews 4:12).

To demolish strongholds, we pray and put on the full armor of God. It's pertinent to note that we can only wield the power of God if we submit to him. If we remain in Christ and Christ remain in us, he said that anything we ask, it will be done for us (John 15:7). We have his full grace when we seek first the kingdom of God and all his righteousness. Fear God and keep his commandments.

Choose the Narrow Path

"This day I call the heavens and the earth as witnesses against you that I have set before you life and death, blessings and curses. Now choose life, so that you and your children may live" (Deuteronomy 30:19).

We all have choices in life. Life isn't as complicated as we make it seem. Choosing to live by God's commands and his wisdom will lead to a prosperous future. Choosing to live by the flesh leads to eternal damnation. The wages of sin is death. The first choice won't be without struggles, but they build perseverance and character. Life is greater when you have God on your side. If God is for you, who can be against you? Choosing to live by the flesh is never truly fulfilling because you only fill your void with temporary things like money and possessions. This simply does not work. There is no amount of money that can truly fill the void God is meant to fill.

Always choose to be spiritually proactive. In whatever season of life you are in, pray for the body of Christ, pray for the lost sheep. Make the choice to be spiritually mature; one cannot be a babe in Christ forever. Wean yourself off the Similac. Think of others outside of yourself and reach out to someone who needs Jesus. Choose to give thanks for everything in your life God has done, is doing, and will do. Ask God to fill you with wisdom, knowledge, and discernment and to guide you with the Holy Spirit. "Enter through the narrow gate. For wide is the gate and broad is the road that leads to destruction, and many enter through it. But small is the gate and narrow the road that leads to life, and only a few find it" (Matthew 7:13-14).

Choose Who You Will Serve

"But if serving the Lord seems undesirable to you, then choose for yourselves this day whom you will serve, whether the gods your ancestors served beyond the Euphrates, or the gods of the Amorites, in whose land you are living. But as for me and my household, we will serve the Lord" (Joshua 24:15).

Every day, we wake up, and we choose whom we will serve. Will it be our self-interests first or the kingdom? We must pray every day for the Lord's people. We must choose whether we will be led by the flesh or the Spirit.

Being led by the flesh means doing what you want to do. It is human nature to be rebellious and engage in behavior that leads to our downfall. Being led by the Spirit means you are crucifying your flesh, and you obey all of God's commands. Romans 8:6-8 says, "The mind governed by the flesh is death, but the mind governed by the Spirit is life and peace. The mind governed by the flesh is hostile to God; it does not submit to God's law, nor can it do so. Those who are in the realm of the flesh cannot please God." Either you live according to the flesh or the Spirit.

Serving the Lord means serving his kingdom. The Lord is a good and compassionate God who is always faithful. If you choose to serve him, nothing can separate you from his Love. "The Lord is my portion; therefore, I will wait for him" (Lamentations 3:24). You can trust him and put it all in his hands. You no longer do things your way; just wait on him. God provides for his children. We must have a strong faith because, without faith, it is impossible to please God. How could you not have faith in a God who sent his only Son to die on the cross for your sins? He's done too many miracles in your life for you to not trust in him. He's already done enough.

Serve the Lord with unwavering faith. Everyone has faith in something; this is evident when you witness people's lives on social media, for example. Many people think they can become the next top model, the next rapper, movie star, or influencer. Faith is the substance of things hoped for, the evidence of things unseen. If worldly people have faith in something that only happens to a small percentage of people, then why can't they have faith in God? Nobody has evidence to prove he DOESN'T exist. People choose to have faith in what they want to have it in. Life is short, and nobody knows the day or hour in which they will pass away, so a decision must be made.

Who will you serve? It isn't complicated. There is only heaven and hell, God and Satan. There is no door number three. As for me and my household, we will serve the Lord (Joshua 24:15).

Deception

After the Israelites were deceived in Joshua chapter 9 by the Gibeonites, they let them become servants in the temple. The reason they were deceived in the first place was because they didn't inquire of the Lord first before making an oath with the Gibeonites. Because the Gibeonites deceived the Israelites, they were under a curse that bound them to be woodcutters and water carriers for the Israelite community. They initially feared for their lives because they knew what the Lord commanded regarding inheriting the land and crushing all of its inhabitants. That fear led them to deceive, but consequently, their lives were put in the Israelites' hands.

There are always consequences when we don't follow God's plan. God was upset that the Israelites brought unbelieving foreigners into his sanctuary. They had a sacred duty to handle the sacrifices, and they let foreigners do it instead.

Now, let's give an example of victory when one listens and does what the Lord says. The king of Jerusalem, Adoni-Zedek, recruited five kings of the Ammonites to attack Gibeon, and the Gibeonites asked the Israelites for their help. God told Joshua not to be afraid and that he would give all his enemies into their hand. "Not one of them will be able to withstand you" (Joshua 10:8).

God went out to fight for them. He threw their enemies

into confusion and rained hail on them. The Lord stopped the sun from going down for a full day to give Joshua and his people more time to fight in daylight. God gave his people the victory, and all their enemies were decimated.

In conclusion, it is better to obey the Lord because you will get the victory every time. Stand firm in the faith and be steadfast. When you face an important decision, put it in God's hands. Don't let the enemy get into your mind and try to steer you wrong. He cannot make you do anything, but he loves to influence you to go against God. Satan masquerades as an angel of light, so his demonic children do as well. Don't be slaves to sin; yet, be slaves to God. Ask him to save and protect you from deceitful lies. He will answer you.

Choose the God you will serve, either the god of this world, or the God who has delivered you from the enemy too many times to count.

Dig your Ditch and Watch God Work

When you need what only the Lord can give, you must have faith that God will deliver it. There are situations that only God's power can fix. He wants us to seek him and rely on him.

When Jehoshaphat, Jehoram, and the king of Edom were marching on their way to defeat Moab (2 Kings 3), they had no water for the troops or the cattle. Water is a human necessity. It is needed to live, and without it, they couldn't fight or survive. Just when Jehoram, the king of Israel, was distressed, Jehoshaphat, the king of Judah, inquired about finding the Lord's prophet. His servant brought up Elisha. They went to Elisha. Elisha told them to dig ditches in the valleys and that water would fill them. Elisha said there wouldn't be wind or rain but that God would provide them with water for them and their cattle to drink. He told them that the Lord would deliver the Moabites into their hands and that they should smite every city, cut down their trees, stone their land, and stop up their wells.

In the morning, as sure as the Lord lives, the ditches were filled with water. The Moabites came to their camp, and they couldn't withstand the Israelites. God provided water for his people and gave their enemies into their hand. Even though Jehoram had done evil in the Lord's sight, Elisha heard them out because Jehoshaphat was with him. "As the Lord of hosts liveth, before whom I stand, surely, were it not that I regard the presence of Jehoshaphat the king of Judah, I would not look toward thee, nor see thee" (v. 14 KJV). God heard Jehoshaphat's prayer and answered.

End Times

"But mark this: There will be terrible times in the last days. People will be lovers of themselves, lovers of money, boastful, proud, abusive, disobedient to their parents, ungrateful, unholy" (2 Timothy 3:1-2).

God gives us warnings throughout the Bible to let us know the end will be near. He tells us to be ready because we will not know the day or the hour Jesus will return. "For the Lord himself will descend from heaven with a cry of command, with the voice of an archangel, and with the sound of the trumpet of God. And the dead in Christ will rise first. Then we who are alive, who are left, will be caught up together with them in the clouds to meet the Lord in the air, and so we will always be with the Lord (1 Thessalonians 4:16-17 ESV).

Only those who are in Christ will be spared from the tribulation and meet the Lord in the air at the appointed time. God is not slow to return according to man's concept of time. He wants everyone to repent and accept Christ. God is trying to give us time to get things right before it's too late. "Be careful, or your hearts will be weighed down with carousing, drunkenness and the anxieties of life, and that day will close on you suddenly like a trap. For it will come on all those who live on the face of the whole earth. Be always on the watch and pray that you may be able to escape all that is about to happen and that you may be able to stand before the Son of Man" (Luke 21:34-36). God is telling us to be careful not to be distracted by all this worldly nonsense because Jesus will return at an hour you will not expect. You need to be ready when he returns.

Many people have this misconception that most people are going to heaven. They either never heard of or don't know the story about Noah. Noah warned everyone about the global flood; meanwhile, by faith, he was building a gigantic ark. Only eight people, including Noah, got on the boat. "For in the days before the flood, people were eating and drinking, marrying and giving in marriage, up to the day Noah entered the ark" (Matthew 24:38).

They are doing the same thing today! There is nothing new under the sun. God said that every thought in man's mind was evil continually, and nothing has changed. We are doing even worse things now, so do not be deceived into thinking most people will go to heaven. When the angels rebelled, God sent them to hell, putting them in chains of darkness to be held for judgment. In Noah's days, he protected the righteous but condemned everyone outside the boat. He condemned Sodom and Gomorrah for their sinful ways but spared Lot, an upright man. This shows that God knows how to rescue the righteous while serving judgment to the lawless. (2 Peter 2:4-10).

If we all could just do what we want to do, then why does hell exist? There are eternal consequences for the decisions we make. Our souls are at stake. This is truly about life or death. God wants us to enter that narrow gate that only a few find. He said that broad is the road and wide is the gate that leads to destruction (Matthew 7:13-14). When your physical body perishes, you will have to account for what was done in this body. People should not deceive themselves about where they stand with God. "Not everyone who says to Me, 'Lord, Lord,' will enter the kingdom of heaven, but he who does the will of My Father who is in heaven. Many will say to Me on that day, 'Lord, Lord, did we not prophesy in Your name, and in your name drive out demons and perform many miracles?' Then I will tell them plainly, 'I never knew you. Away from me, you evil-doers!'" (Matthew 7:21-23).

The bottom line is that when it is all said and done, one should want to be in that Lamb's book of Life (Rev. 21:27). Those who have accepted Christ, repented of their sins, and are walking with him are in the book of life. There is only one book because many are called, but few are chosen. Most have gone their own way. But there are multiple books that will be opened, and the unsaved will be judged. Revelation 20:12-15 sums it up: "And I saw the dead, great and small, standing before the throne, and books were opened. Another book was opened, which is the Book of Life. The dead were judged according to what they had done, as recorded in the books. The sea gave up the dead that were in it, and death and Hades gave up the dead that were in them, and each person was judged according to what they had done. Then, death and Hades were thrown into the lake of fire. The lake of fire is the second death. Anyone whose name was not found written in the Book of Life was thrown into the lake of fire."

Endurance

Habakkuk, the prophet God sent to warn the Israelites, told them they would be humbled because of their stiff-necked ways. God had already sent many prophets during previous generations to warn them. During this time, the Babylonians had conquered them, but Habakkuk didn't lose faith. He said that the decay crept in his bones, the olive crops failed, there were no grapes on the vine, and there was no food. But he still said, "Yet I will rejoice in the Lord, I will be joyful in God my Savior" (Habakkuk 3:18).

God is God. He is *I am*. He makes his plans, and who are we to ask him to go easy on us? Who is God that he needs someone to counsel him? God disciplines those whom he loves. We must endure patiently. "Yet I will wait patiently for the day of calamity to come on the nation invading us" (v. 16). Be patient and trust in God's plans. He will never put more on you than you can bear. "The sovereign Lord is my strength; He makes my feet like the feet of a deer; he enables me to tread on the heights" (v. 19). God gives you the strength to endure anything. You can and will stand firm against the enemy.

Envy

"For where you have envy and selfish ambition, there you find disorder and every evil practice" (James 3:16).

Remember, everything good and pure comes from the Lord, but putting self-interest first is from the evil one. Selfishness, being covetous, and being boastful are not of God. Do not be of the world, even though you live in it. Let the wisdom that comes from God be shown through good deeds done in humility. Surrender to God, put him first, and he will impart wisdom to you. Trust in him and rely on him, not your own understanding.

Focus on God's plan for your life and the blessings he has for you. God cannot bless you while you are being envious of others. What is for you is for you. You should put self-interest last and be more Christ-like. Jesus' entire life was about helping and sacrificing for others. If we focused more on doing our jobs as fishers of men, then we wouldn't get sidetracked by being envious of other people's lives. God said if you sought his kingdom first and kept his commandments, he would give you the desires of your heart.

So, if you have faith, and you are taking care of God's business, then he will take care of yours. If you can admit you have envy in your heart, repent right now and ask God to take away from you what is not of him. When God knows you have a sincere heart, he listens. God only hears the prayers of the righteous and the repentant. To truly walk with the Lord, one must recognize the parts of them that need to be pruned. If you accept Christ as your Savior, repent of your sins, and become a new creature, then the former things shall pass away. That does not mean you will never fall short of God's glory. But you cannot go on sinning and making excuses. Once you have sinned, you repent sincerely and put on the full armor of God so you won't commit that same particular sin again.

Faith in Battle

"'Don't be afraid,' the Prophet answered. 'Those who are with us are more than those who are with them'" (2 Kings 6:16).

It's easy to look at things with the naked eye and worry because you can't see what God is doing. You can't focus on what you can physically see, but you must trust in God's plan. Have faith that having God on your side beats the god of this world every time. "'Open his eyes, Lord, so that he may see.' Then the Lord opened the servant's eyes, and he looked and saw the hills full of horses and chariots of fire all around Elisha" (v. 17). We need to open our spiritual eyes to what God is doing. Once we do that, we, too, will see that there are chariots of fire surrounding us, protecting us.

We need to extend to our enemies the same grace that has been given to us. Elisha asks God to make the Aramaean army blind. Most people would have wished them dead. Instead, Elisha led the blind army to Samaria to feed them. The king of Israel asked if he should kill them; Elisha told him no. We can learn a valuable lesson from Elisha, the Prophet. Trust in God's power and be kind to your enemies. When you align your will with God's and do your best to have a godly character, God will be with you. Elisha wasn't worried about the Aramaeans. He understood that the war wasn't against flesh and blood; it was against the dark spiritual forces, the principalities, the powers of the dark world, and the authorities and rulers. But he knew that the almighty God was on his side. With God on our side, who can be against us? The same God that gave his only Son will graciously give us what we ask according to his will. We are conquerors in Christ, and nothing can separate us from the love of God that is in Christ Jesus our Lord (Romans 8:38-39).

Fear

"However, I consider my life worth nothing to me, if only I may finish the race and complete the task the Lord Jesus has given me—the task of testifying to the gospel of God's grace" (Acts 20:24).

Don't let the fear of failure prevent you from doing what God has called you to do. No matter what season of life you are in, you have a responsibility to the world. We are to go out to the world and advance the gospel. Encourage your brothers and sisters in Christ and help strengthen their faith. Use the gift God gave you to build up the kingdom of God. If we stand firm in the faith till the end, we will inherit the kingdom of heaven. Paul says in Romans to be humble and not prideful with your gifts. According to one's faith, use one's gift cheerfully, whether it's serving, teaching, prophesying, encouraging, giving, etc. We are all members of Christ's body, and we all have a separate function. The mission is to educate, engage, equip, and evangelize for the kingdom of God.

In 1 Peter 4:10, Peter drove the point home about using your gifts "to serve others as faithful stewards of God's grace in its various forms." We must do so "with the strength God provides" (v. 11). God is glorified through Jesus Christ. Focus on God. "Many are the plans in a person's heart, but it is the Lord's purpose that prevails" (Proverbs 19:21). Don't let fear cripple you from moving into your purpose. God did not give you a spirit of fear. Satan is not afraid of advancing his cause, so why should a warrior in Christ be fearful of advancing the gospel? The Spirit God gave us does not make us timid, but gives us power, love, and self-discipline" (2 Timothy 1:7).

We were made to live courageously the life God ordained for us. Fear and faith are opposites of each other. With faith in God, you do not operate with fear. We know that faith is essential because, without it, it is impossible to please God. God calls you to be a courageous warrior with a strong faith. He wants us to be obedient as well, which means we have self-control and discipline. We can have power, love, and self-control because God helps us with these things. We are new creatures doing a new thing. Having a fearful spirit is the old you. We are now born-again co-heirs with Christ. Love drives out fear, so if you operate on fear, you don't have perfect love. "The one who fears is not made in perfect love" (1 John 4:18). Yield your ways and will to the Lord. There is peace in obedience. We are to be bold for Christ and on fire for the Lord and his kingdom. You are the one holding yourself back. Let God work on your timidity, fear, and desire to be a "safe" Christ servant.

Fighting the Flesh

"Watch and pray so that you will not fall into temptation. The Spirit is willing, but the body is weak" (Matthew 26:41).

Know what your weaknesses are so you can work on them and ask God for his assistance. God will strengthen you where you are weak. For example, if you know you can be overly emotional, ask God to help you gain control over your emotions. Since we are naturally rebellious, it's easy to give in at times. We must do what Christ did. He often would go away by himself and pray to Father God. God already knows where we are weak; he is just waiting for us to come to him. We must lean on him and let his power rest on us. We cannot do it on our own.

We do not have a high priest who can't relate to what we go through (Hebrews 4:15). He went through more than we can ever imagine, yet he did not sin. Jesus had fasted for forty days and nights in the desert and was hungry when Satan tempted him. He told Jesus to make stones turn into bread. But Jesus used his sword, the Word of God, against him. He told the adversary that man must not live on bread alone but on every word that comes from the mouth of God. At that point, Satan took him to the holy city, told him to stand on the highest point, and said that God would command his angels concerning him. Jesus told him, "Do not put the Lord your God to the test."

Last, Satan told him to bow down and worship him, promising him all the kingdoms of the world. Jesus told him that the Word says to worship the Lord your God and serve him only. Then the devil left him.

Jesus also experienced sorrowful moments. When he was about to be crucified, he prayed, "May this cup be taken from me." He returned to his disciples and told them to keep watch and pray. He went away again and prayed to God, "If it's not possible for this cup to be taken away from me unless I drink it, let your will be done."

When emotions are high, do what Jesus did; go away and pray to the Father. God is in control. Thank God for the grace that we received through Jesus Christ. Jesus intercedes for us. We just need to come to him in all situations.

We must also do our part. We should not intentionally put ourselves in situations where we know there will be temptation. Instead, we must align our ways with the Word of God. God will never allow us to be tempted beyond what we can handle. He will allow us a way to escape. But the key is, we must WANT to resist temptation.

Paul said he boasts about his weaknesses so that Christ's power would rest on him. He delighted in insults, hardships, persecutions, and difficulties, "For when I am weak, then I am strong" (2 Corinthians 12:10). Christ's power and grace are sufficient for us. He can handle all your shortcomings.

Focus on the Eternal

It is rather easy to get caught up in securing a comfortable life on earth. Everyone wants a good job or career. Everyone wants to travel. Everyone wants to look good on social media. You can't get caught up in what is temporary. You must choose whom you will serve. Will you serve God or your fleshly desires? The decision you make will determine what happens after taking your last breath. You will either enjoy eternal life in paradise or eternal death in the lake of fire. What's the point of doing things your way when it will cost you your soul? "What good is it for someone to gain the whole world yet forfeit their soul? Or what can anyone give in exchange for their soul?" (Mark 8:36-37).

If you chase money in this life, you can't take it with you, plus you will suffer eternally by fire. Think about it like this: we are only on this earth for a brief time, yet we will sacrifice paradise to do what we want to do. Eternity is a hefty price tag to gamble with. Living according to God's will leads to eternal paradise. It sounds simple, but we make it more difficult than it should be.

Don't store up for yourself treasures on earth. It doesn't last, for everything will pass away. If you store for yourselves treasures in heaven, it can't be taken away. "For where your treasure is, there your heart will be also" (Matthew 6:21). Let sacrificing for God's people be your treasure, not spreading debauchery on this earth. There are two paths. One leads to life. One leads to death.

Forgive and Watch God Elevate You

Whatever position you are currently in right now, thank God for it. Everything is working together for your good. Maybe you can't see it now, and you are losing patience and hope. Stand firm because God has perfect timing. He can even use someone else's betrayal to lead you toward a major blessing.

Consider Joseph in Genesis 39. His brothers sold him into slavery, but God was still with him. "But while Joseph was there in the prison, the Lord was with him. He showed him kindness and granted him favor in the eyes of the prison warden" (v. 21). Joseph went from being sold to the Midianites to being Potiphar's servant to being accused of sleeping with Potiphar's wife and being thrown into prison, leading him to gain favor with the warden. The Lord gave him success with everything that he did.

Because Joseph correctly interpreted a dream for Pharaoh's cupbearer, years later, the Pharaoh asked Joseph to interpret his dream. Since Joseph was the only one there with the Spirit of God who could interpret, Pharaoh made him second-in-command over the kingdom. God helped him forget about all those previous troubling years. He then got married and had kids.

Years later, Joseph and his brothers' paths crossed. They

threw themselves at his feet in mercy, but Joseph wasn't upset. He didn't hold a grudge. "You intended to harm me, but God intended it for good to accomplish what is now being done, the saving of many lives" (Genesis 50:20). The bad that was done to Joseph led to him overseeing Egypt. He sold the grain. It was the same grain that his brothers would need during the famine. God can put you in a position to bless the very ones who wronged you and, at the same time, elevate you to save many lives.

Joseph was sold at seventeen years old and was made a ruler at thirty. God turned it around for his good. Your current situation is not your destination. God has a plan and can do immeasurably more than you can ever ask or imagine. The first will be last, and the last will be first; Jesus humbled himself as a servant on earth, and God exalted him to the highest place and gave him a name above every name. When you walk with God and humble yourself, there will be a great reward in the end. "Be kind and compassionate to one another, forgiving each other just as in Christ God forgave you" (Ephesians 4:32).

Do unto others as you would have them do unto you. Treating others the way Christ would can be a challenge, especially when they have wronged you. We cannot focus on the trespass because God said that our transgressions are as far as the east is from the west. When God forgives us for something, he doesn't hold it against us. We repent, and it is erased. Understandably, human beings are sometimes not apologetic, offering no remorse for their actions. But even when someone sins against us and is not sorry, we still must forgive. It hurts us to hold grudges. God really wants us to forgive. This is illustrated in Luke 17:4: "Even if they sin against you seven times in a day and seven times come back to you saying, 'I repent,' you must forgive them."

We are to exemplify Christ in how we love and show forgiveness. Let go of that burden. Jesus tells a parable about two men owing money to a lender. One man owed little, while the other owed much. The lender forgave both since they didn't have the money. Jesus asks which one loved the lender more. The answer was the one with the larger debt. "But whoever has been forgiven little loves little" (Luke 7:47). I know that in my case, God has forgiven me for many things. And I'm very thankful for his mercy. I must return the favor to my neighbor. They will be thankful for all I have forgiven them for.

Gifts and Good Works

"For we are God's workmanship, created in Christ Jesus to do good works, which God prepared in advance for us to do" (Ephesians 2:10).

God knew everything that would happen before it came to be. All our experiences in life have shaped us. We must use our testimony to bring others to Christ. We are given gifts, passions, and personalities from God. We need to use them as workers in the harvest and not sit on our gifts. Peter said, "Each one should use whatever gift he has received to serve others, faithfully administering God's grace in its various forms" (1 Peter 4:10).

Give to your neighbor. By serving others, you are serving Christ. Matthew 25:40 says, "Truly I tell you, whatever you did for one of the least of these brothers and sisters of mine, you did for me." Put all people before yourself. Treat your neighbor the way you would want to be treated. Ask God to reveal your gifts and use them faithfully. Speak the Word of God. Serve with the strength God gave you. Be zealous in doing the work for the kingdom. All things work together for the good of those who love him and who are called according to his purpose. God has a purpose for your life. He gave you a gift so that while you are on this earth, you can serve others. You are his vessel to carry out the earthly task of planting seeds of righteousness.

Giving

It is better to give than to receive. In the New Testament, Jesus constantly shows us examples of blessing others. He performs numerous miracles and heals the sick. He even raised Lazarus from the dead. He broke bread and fish for the five thousand. Jesus always gave. We are supposed to follow his example. We might not be able to touch someone to heal cancer or raise someone from the dead, but we can give our prayers, time, resources, energy, food, and wise counsel to someone in need. There is always someone who needs something. The Word says there will always be the poor among you.

As children of God, we are called to be meek and humble. Instead of expecting material things and gifts, be more generous. Be a cheerful giver on this earth. Give in secret so that the Father, who sees what was done in secret, will reward you. The exalted will be humbled, and the humbled will be exalted. When you are sitting at a dinner party, sit at the lowest place (Luke 14:10). Build others up with encouraging words. Don't always think about yourself and your self-interests. Instead of asking God what he can do for you, ask yourself what you can sacrifice for God.

The greatest gift of all time was God giving his only Son, that whoever believes in him shall not perish but have eternal life (John 3:16). He gave his son while we were yet sinners so that we would not perish if we believed in him.

That is the greatest gift of love. We were made in God's image, and we are to model our lives after him. Jesus said we would do even greater things than he because he was going to the Father. Give back what God has blessed you with.

God has a Future for You

"There is surely a future hope for you, and your hope will not be cut off" (Proverbs 23:18).

When you share in Jesus' suffering for his sake, you will also share in his everlasting glory. Now that you are doing a new thing, you learn that Jesus' yoke is light and easy. But because you are a child of God living in a fallen world, there will be trials and tribulations. But count it pure joy when you encounter struggles, because the trying of your faith creates patience. (James 1:3-4). Blessed is the one who endures temptation, for he shall receive eternal life in the end. God's will for you includes exhibiting the fruit of the Spirit (Galatians 5:22-23), taking up your cross (Matthew 16:24), losing your life for Jesus' sake to find it (Matthew 10:39), and obedience (1 John 5:3).

Surrender it all to God, and he will guide your steps. Do a new thing and watch it spring forth. It will take some confessions and humility to grow with God. Don't get too prideful to admit when you fall short. You are nothing without God. Your life is only a passing vapor on this earth. The Spirit is willing, but the flesh is weak. God knows what you've done already; he is just waiting for you to come to him and repent. He is the Father, and he wants us to come to him like little children. He can deliver you and wipe your soul clean. Your transgressions are as far as the east is from the west. Live the life God called you to live. Submit to his authority, humble yourself before God, and watch him do great things in your life.

God Will Fill Thy Cup

When the prophet's widow cried because the creditors were going to take her sons, the Lord provided. Elisha, a prophet of the Lord, asked her, "What hast thou in the house?" (2 Kings 4:2). The widow told him she only had a jar of oil. He told her to borrow jars from all her neighbors and to fill up each jar until full. She was able to fill each jar; not one was left empty. When she went back to Elisha, he told her to sell all the jars, pay off her debt, and live off the rest.

God can use whatever little you have and multiply it. He can and will provide all that you need. All things work together for the good of those who love him. He will not allow you to go without. He is a faithful God.

In the Word of God, there are many examples of God taking very little and doing a lot. Jesus took a few loaves of bread and fish and fed 5,000 men, women, and children. God allowed David to beat the giant Goliath, despite David being just a young ruddy boy. Through the power of God, a few troops of Israelites defeated large armies. He is able to deliver you from any situation. Faith is paramount in your relationship with God. You must believe he exists and that he rewards those who diligently seek him.

God's Plan

Stop questioning God's plan for your life. Just surrender to him, knowing he knows best,

The pottery can't question the potter who formed it. We often see things from our human perspective, and it gets easy to be frustrated. Do not try to enter logic into the equation. Just trust in him. "As the heavens are higher than the earth, so are my ways higher than your ways and my thoughts than your thoughts" (Isaiah 55:9). God is not like us. He doesn't think like us. God is *I am*. A thousand years with the Lord are like a day, and a day with him is like a thousand years. Let God handle your problems. Let him lead your life. Don't say what you plan to do next year or five years from now. It will happen only if it is God's will.

Surrender your plans to God. Put your trust in him because he has your best interest at heart. He has plans to prosper you, not to harm you, plans to give you hope and a future (Jeremiah 29:11). When you fully surrender to God, you no longer live for yourself; you live for him. God wants you to follow his commands and not just be readers of the Word but also doers. Your fleshly self has died. You no longer do what the world does. You are a new creature. God wants you to worship him and testify about what he's done for you. Your whole duty on this earth is to spread the gospel, follow his commandments, and fear God. "I have been crucified with Christ and no longer live, but Christ lives in me. The life I now live in the body, I live by faith in the Son of God, who loved me and gave himself for me" (Galatians 2:20).

Guard Your Heart

"Above all else, guard your heart, for everything you do flows from it" (Proverbs 4:23).

Everything we consume affects our heart. The music we listen to, the movies we watch, and the conversations we have all affect our hearts. You are what you eat. The wretched music you constantly listen to is negatively influencing you. The rated R movies with extreme violence and sexual situations put thoughts into your head. It is no secret that many wayward teenagers who commit crimes have stated that they played violent graphic video games. It is important that, as children of God, we are careful about what we consume. "For where your treasure is, there your heart will be also" (Luke 12:34). Constantly scrolling through social media and looking at other people's lives can lead to gossip and/or envy. It also promotes being busybodies in other people's business. 1 Peter 4:15 (KJ21) says, "But let none of you suffer as a murderer, or *as* a thief, or *as* an evildoer, or as a busybody in other men's matters." We must be cognizant of what TV we consume, the type of music we enjoy, the social media we engage with, the video games we play, and the people we associate with. The last part of verse 23 says, "For everything you do flows from it." Whatever you put in will come out. If you feed your spirit junk, then junk will flow out. If you feed it holiness, praise, the Word, and all things admirable, then that's what you will give out.

Having Patience and Faith in the Promise

In Genesis 16, Sarah and Abraham took matters into their own hands. God told them he would give them an heir and make him the father of a great nation. They got impatient and hatched a plan to give Abraham an heir through Hagar. We often try to take matters into our own hands, but God doesn't need any help from us.

However, God is so good that he takes our illegitimate plans and still uses them for our good. He had a plan for Hagar's son from Abraham. "And as for Ishmael, I have heard you: I will surely bless him; I will make him fruitful and will greatly increase his numbers. He will be the father of twelve rulers, and I will make him into a great nation" (Genesis 17:20). God doesn't do this for every person, though. God chooses whom to have mercy on and whom to bless according to his perfect will. We are to be patient children who follow God's commandments while he does the work in our lives.

A promise is a promise, and God is a promise keeper. Have faith that God will do what he said he would do. God does not operate on our timing. It is human nature to want things to happen when we want them to happen. The Word says his ways are not our ways and his thoughts are not our thoughts. We must operate on faith. It is the evidence of things unseen. "Now faith is confidence in what we hope for and assurance about what we do not see" (Hebrews 11:1). We might not see evidence of the promise, yet faith is still believing it will happen.

He is an On-Time God

"There is a time to love and a time to hate, a time for war and a time for peace" (Ecclesiastes 3:8).

God has perfect timing for every situation. Our impatience brings us discomfort. We need to trust and have faith in God's timing.

For example, when desiring a spouse, God said there is a time to love. He knows certain things must happen first before he sends a blessing. We must mature, grow spiritually, gain knowledge, and ultimately become the godly person who deserves a spouse. When we are ready, God will send him or her if it is in his will. Not everyone will get married. "He has made everything beautiful in its time" (Ecclesiastes 3:11). Let God refine you and prepare you for your blessing.

If you have been waiting for a promotion from your job for years and you are losing hope, God has plans for your life. He wants you to prosper. "Many are the plans in a man's heart, but it the Lord's purpose that prevails" (Proverbs 19:21). We can say all day what job we plan to have, where we want to live, what car we will buy, but God has an intentional purpose for our lives, and we shouldn't try to derail it. We must have the fruit of the Spirit, which includes patience.

Show your faith by acting as if you've already received the blessing. Let God know you believe in his awesome power. Let his will be done according to his perfect timing.

His Perfect Timing

"When Abraham was 99 years old, the Lord appeared to him and said, 'I am God Almighty; walk before me faithfully and be blameless. Then I will make my covenant between me and you and will greatly increase your numbers'" (Genesis 17:1-2).

God can do anything. Through him, everything was made. He has all the power, and it belongs to him. If we are faithful and walk with God, he will bless us beyond measure. He keeps his promises just like he kept the covenant with the Israelites. Abraham was 99 years old when God made the covenant with him. God promised Abraham and Sarah a son even though Sarah was ninety years old. God does things in his own time according to his will. Sarah having a child at ninety is evidence that with God, all things are possible.

Never be impatient about what God is going to do in your life. "But do not forget this one thing, dear friends: With the Lord, a day is like 1000 years, and 1000 years are like a day. The Lord is not slow in keeping his promise, as some understand slowness. Instead, he is patient with you, not wanting anyone to perish, but everyone to come to repentance" (2 Peter 3:8-9). God doesn't have the same concept of time as humans. Our ways are not his ways. He is the creator. God is patient with us because he wants us to prosper, not perish. Trust in the Lord's promises. Be patient and have faith that

God is able and willing to do immeasurably more than we could ask or imagine, according to his power that is at work within us!

Hope

"But those who hope in the Lord will renew their strength. They will soar on wings like eagles; they will run and not grow weary; they will walk and not grow faint" (Isaiah 40:31).

Don't dwell on the past. Don't think about what isn't going your way. Guard your heart in Christ Jesus. Rely on God's strength to get you through every situation. He wants you to lean on him. Don't lean on your own understanding. The enemy will try to creep in and convince you that you are unworthy because of your past. Remind yourself of who you are in Christ. Do not listen to the lies. Satan is the father of lies. Meditate on God's Word, "the word of our God stands forever" (Isaiah 40:8).

The situations we endure on this earth are temporary. Fix your mind on heavenly things above. We are to enjoy our short time on earth while serving God and letting his will be done. It is God's gift that we pursue a passion in life. Whatever you do, give glory to God while doing it. Our purpose on earth is to help bring others to the kingdom and to use our gifts to praise and glorify his name. Everything else is just an extra blessing from God. He allows us to have an education, a career, and a family. We plant seeds of righteousness; someone else may water them, but it is God who saves them. God is in control, and he has sovereign power.

He is trustworthy and faithful and brings justice. "Like a shepherd leading his flock, he makes us a straight path. He gathers the lambs in his arms and carries them close to his heart" (Isaiah 40:11).

Have hope because he gives strength to the weary. Faith is the key to hope. Faith is the evidence of things unseen, so one must have faith to hope for a future. He is a faithful God that has the power to sustain you. He wants your soul to prosper. There is hope in keeping God's promises in your heart. Know he is able and willing to complete a good work in you. Needing physical evidence to believe is the opposite of hope. A hope that is seen is no hope at all. Without hope, you cannot move forward. The adversary wants you to stay in a hopeless state because if you are hopeless and feeling depressed, you can't advance the kingdom. There is no need to worry or feel anxious because God has already done a great thing. He sent his son Jesus Christ, the Lamb of God, as a sacrifice for our sins. That alone is the great news that gives everlasting hope. By him just waking you up another day is enough hope to let you know God loves you.

He wants the best for you, and he wants you to stand firm till the end so that you may receive your inheritance. As a child of God, you have many benefits. He is a living God that always hears you. He loves you and will never forsake you. He is the same God that created the heavens and the earth, the sun, moon, and stars. He even knows the number of hairs on our head. Give thanks for all he has done for you, and put all your trust, faith, and hope in him. "Against all hope, Abraham in hope believed and so became the father of many nations, just as it has been said to him, 'So shall your offspring be'" (Romans 4:18). Abraham knew he was old and his body was breaking down, but he believed what God told him. He remembered God's promises. His faith was credited to him as righteousness. It wasn't good works that justified him. When we go to work, we aren't praised for it. It is something we are supposed to do. It is an obligation. When we trust God and have faith in him, that faith is credited to us as righteousness.

Our transgressions were forgiven when Jesus died on the cross. We must believe that through Jesus's blood, we are saved. In Luke 18:27, Jesus replied, "What is impossible with men is possible with God." Anything that seems to be too farfetched or unrealistic, God can work out. He can make the unlikeliest situations happen. He has the power. He can give you a job you don't qualify for. He can get a bill paid when you don't have the money for it. He can heal a disease the doctors don't have a cure for. He can give a baby to a woman forty years past her fertile period. There are things beyond human control that God will take control of. When there is a plan for your life, he will make sure everything aligns to fulfill his will for you. He can make a way out of no way.

James chapter 5 talks about how the righteous are powerful. When a person is sick, they could be anointed with oil and prayed over by men walking with God. Prayers of the righteous are effective. "Confess your sins and pray for each other" (v. 16). Just like in Matthew 9:2-6, Jesus saw the paralyzed man and forgave his sins because he wanted to demonstrate he had the authority to do so. He forgave him and told him to get up and walk. The man got up and walked home.

'

How Can We Be More Like God?

"Follow God's example, therefore, as dearly loved children and walk in the way of love, just as Christ loved us and gave himself up for us as a fragrant offering and sacrifice to God" (Ephesians 5:1-2).

Instead of focusing on beauty, material possessions, social or economic status, focus on God. Focus on being grateful and give thanks to the creator. Jesus told us the exalted will be humbled, and the humbled will be exalted. Jesus gave his life for us so we would have eternal life. That is the greatest example of putting others above yourself. Applying these principles to our lives is God's will for us. We need to do unto others as we would have them do unto us. Every day is a chance to follow God's example. Sacrifice for someone else and give generously. Whether it be money, time, food, shelter, or wise counsel, be a cheerful giver to your neighbor. Don't fix your mind on outside beauty, for God looks at the heart. Above all, love one another as God loves you. Love conquers all and does not fail.

As Christ-filled servants, if we are busy studying the Word, praising him, doing good works, and being a cheerful giver, we won't be distracted by what the world offers. The world tells society to care about looks, lustful desires, money, material things, or moving up the corporate ladder, but Christ's ambassadors know what life is truly about. Life is more than a job. Life is more than going to the gym to look like an Instagram model. We were put on this earth to serve God, proclaim the good news to the world, and do great works. Leave everything else in God's hands.

Pray and have faith he will provide. God has plans to prosper you and make your life abundant in the spiritual sense, not in a worldly way. Following God's example means to keep the light inside of you lit. Nobody hides a lamp; rather, they keep it lit and place it on a stand for everyone to see. You are an example to the world. Moreover, just like Satan wanted to thwart God's plans, he will try to thwart your mission. He hates that you are a new creature walking with God. His mission is to snuff your light and encourage you to disobey the creator.

That is what he did to Eve. All he did was convince her that by eating the fruit, she would know good and evil and be like God. In doing this, she ate the fruit and disobeyed God. Satan's mission has never changed. He wants to convince you to disobey so you can be with him and erase your name from the Lamb's Book of Life. Don't let the enemy win. Put on the full armor of God, and you will have the victory. God has already won; he just needs you to stand firm till the end and take hold of your inheritance.

Humility

In 2 Kings 5, Naaman, a commander of the army of the king of Aram, had leprosy. A servant girl urged him to seek out the prophet Elisha in Samaria so he could be healed. Naaman sent a letter to the king of Israel about his leprosy. The king tore his robes, and when Elisha heard of this, he had Naaman sent to him. When Naaman made it to Elisha, Elisha told him to dip himself in the Jordan River seven times and he would be restored. At first, Naaman was angry and expected his healing to be done through some great majestic gesture. But after his servants convinced him, he then dipped himself in the Jordan seven times, and he was renewed. His skin was like that of a young man. He then proclaimed, "There is no God in all the world except in Israel" (2 Kings 5:15). He then refused to make burnt offerings to any other god.

Naaman was like many people today. He wanted his blessing the way he wanted. When we expect a miracle, we can't tell God how to do it. His ways are not our ways. Just have faith in the process. Put your trust in God and lean not into your own understanding (Proverbs 3:5). God is faithful and doesn't need our help. Let God direct your path and he will bless you in his perfect timing.

We need to humble ourselves and give it all to God. Cast your cares onto him because he cares for you. You are not Superman, and you cannot do anything apart from God. It is God who wakes you up every morning. It is by his strength and power that you have made it thus far. Acknowledge him in all your ways and give credit where it is due. Our bodies are nothing but lumps of clay that will eventually turn to dust in the end. We are all going to pass away one day, no matter our earthly net worth or the political party we may choose to identify with.

Idolatry

"You shall have no other gods before me. You shall not make for yourself an image in the form of anything in heaven above or on the earth beneath or in the waters below. You shall not bow down to them or worship them; for I, the Lord your God, am a jealous God, punishing the children for the sin of the parents to the third and fourth generation of those who hate me" (Exodus 20:3-5).

You are not to worship anything other than God, including human beings, material possessions, or your job. God is to be put first, and he is a jealous God. He is the one responsible for waking you up this morning, performing miracles in your life, giving you wisdom and knowledge, healing you, and answering your prayers. He blesses you and plans to give you hope and a future. That Birkin bag can't heal you. Those pairs of Christian Louboutin's can't redeem you from your sins. You won't go to heaven by worshipping a big house or an executive job. The boyfriend/girlfriend doesn't have the power to put you in heaven or hell. It was God who sent his only begotten Son to earth to die for our sins. Seek ye first the kingdom of God and his righteousness, and all these things shall be added unto you.

Do not be like the Israelites, who built the golden calf after God delivered them from the Egyptians. God did so many miraculous things for them, yet they still worshipped an inanimate object. Many people make idols out of material things or even out of other people. Some make marriage or their children an idol. God is not to be mocked. Worship the Lord your God and serve him only.

Isolation

During the pandemic, our lifestyles were drastically altered. It was a season where old friends distanced themselves from us. Some of us were working from home. We weren't doing things we would normally do before the pandemic. Or maybe we were surrounded by friends, but it still felt like a lonely season.

Let's consider Elijah, one of the Lord's Old Testament prophets (1 Kings chapters 17-19). Through Elijah, the Lord told King Ahab that there wouldn't be rain for years except at his word. Afterwards, God told Elijah to leave there and hide in the Kerith Ravine. He told him to drink from the brook, and the ravens would feed him. So, Elijah did what the Lord said. The ravens fed him in the morning and evening as promised. In this time of isolation, Elijah was never really by himself. God was with him the entire time, being a provider. During this moment of isolation, God was preparing Elijah for great things. God does his greatest work when you are by yourself.

Later in chapter 17, it is revealed that Elijah cried out to the Lord to restore the life of a widow's son, and God restored the boy's life. The widow told him, "I know you are a man of God and that the word of the Lord from your mouth is the truth" (17:24). God glorified his name by restoring the boy's life.

Then God spoke to Elijah years later, telling him it would

rain again once he presented himself to King Ahab. Now, on Mount Carmel, Elijah challenged the followers of the false god Baal to prove their gods' power by burning a bull sacrifice. He told them he would show his Lord's power, and whoever's god answered by fire is the one true living God. When the Baal followers danced and prophesied, nothing happened. Elijah prayed to God to let it be known that his God was the God of Israel and that everything he said was by God's command. Immediately, the fire of the Lord burned up his bull sacrifice. When the Baal followers saw this, they bowed down and cried, "He is God."

Meanwhile, Elijah killed all the Baal prophets, but Ahab and Jezebel were angry at this. Elijah ran for his life and was afraid. He prayed he would just die. An angel then appeared and told him to get up and eat. There was food beside him. Strengthened, he traveled forty days and forty nights until he reached Horeb, the mountain of God. God told him to stand on the mountain and await the presence of the Lord. Elijah told him he had been zealous for God but that he was the last prophet left, and there were plans to end his life. God then tells him to go to the desert of Damascus to anoint Aram, the new king over Israel, and anoint Elisha, the prophet, to succeed him.

God did many amazing things through Elijah. Elijah did not have a fraternity with him. He had no coworkers to keep him company. He didn't have a girlfriend. He wasn't meeting up with people through social media networks. He wasn't going on cruises or beach getaways. He was by himself, but God chose him to accomplish great things. God must get us by ourselves at times to do his best work on us and through us. We may not be a part of friendship groups as portrayed in movies such as *The Hangover* or *Girls Trip*, but we are doing something more important: serving the Lord. God needs us to be focused while we are on our mission. When the desire arises for leisure trips with friends and family, just think about Elijah alone in the Kerith Ravine, but God still provided what he needed. We must be reminded that life is not always about having fun and doing what we want to do all the time. Remember why we are here. Ecclesiastes 12:13 says to fear God and keep his commandments. Nothing is wrong with leisure trips when deserved, but sometimes it isn't possible, or there is no one to go with. In those times, just remember that God is still faithful. People alone do not sustain you; God does. He knows what he is doing. Put your trust and hope in the Lord.

Jesus Understands

"Because he himself suffered when he was tempted, he is able to help those who are being tempted" (Hebrews 2:18).

There is nothing we have been through that Jesus hasn't overcome. Jesus walked the earth in his human form, being tempted just like we are today. He showed us that using the Word is our weapon against Satan. Christ's life is an example of how to live on this earth. Just like Jesus, we need to use the Word to fight the enemy's advances. Let nobody try to tell you it is impossible to live a perfect, righteous life. Don't let the world lie to you and say, "Well, nobody is perfect," or "I'm only human." They just use excuses so they can do what they want to do. Jesus showed us it is possible to live a righteous life. The difference between Jesus and those who walk with God is Jesus never sinned. However, we were born into sin, and once we accepted Jesus into our hearts and confessed Jesus Christ is Lord, we became new creatures, children of God. We are expected to live righteously as Jesus did.

When temptation knocks on your door, you have the tools available to make Satan flee. With God's power through his Word, you can stand strong just like Jesus did. "For we do not have a high priest who is unable to empathize with our weakness, but we have one who has been tempted in every way, just as we are—yet he did not sin" (Hebrews 4:15). Jesus understands what we go through. He overcame it all. We can rely on him to help us during a tough time. No temptation has overtaken you except what is common to mankind. And God is faithful; he will not let you be tempted beyond what you can bear (1 Corinthians 10:13).

Satan must get permission from God to test you in the same way that Satan received permission from God to test Job. In Job chapter 2, Satan talks about roaming across the earth. God then asks Satan if he has considered Job, who lived a holy, righteous life, blameless and upright. Satan responds that a man will do anything for his own life and that if Job's good health was taken away, surely Job would curse God. The Lord responds that Satan had permission to do to Job what he pleases but to spare Job's life.

Rest in the fact that if the enemy is testing you, it means you are walking upright. And the enemy cannot destroy you. God is the one in control and he said he would never leave you nor forsake you.

Don't let the enemy win. Man must not live on bread alone but on every word from the mouth of God.

Jesus Yoke

"Come to me, all you who are weary and burdened, and I will give you rest" (Matthew 11:28-30).

This speaks to us who are tired and trying to handle things on our own. It is burdensome when we try to do things our own way. Jesus asks us to come to him, and he will take the burden. "Take my yoke upon you and learn from me, for I am gentle and humble in heart, and you will find rest for your souls" (v. 29). Jesus tells us to be like him, humble and meek. To be like him and learn from his life, we will get rest for our souls. "For my yoke is easy and my burden is light" (v. 30). Jesus is saying that serving and obeying God's will makes life easier. This doesn't mean there won't be struggles, but with God on your side, you can conquer anything.

I can testify that doing things God's way is much easier and stress-free. I've never been more at peace in my life. Living a life full of sin made me internally miserable and depressed. On the outside, it may seem sinners are "living their best life," but they are empty. When they get alone by themselves at night, only they, God, and the devil know what's truly going on in their hearts, minds, and souls. They are deceiving themselves.

Many people go through life without a guide, and they make up things as they go. This unpredictable way of life can be difficult and unfulfilling. They are not truly happy or content. If they were content, they wouldn't have to post constantly on social media to get attention from strangers or go on dating apps for hookups. Once you surrender to God, you have an advocate, the Holy Spirit. And you have an instructional guide, the Word of God, that has wisdom for every situation under the sun.

Keep Your Lamp Lit

"May the favor of the Lord our God rest on us; establish the work of our hands for us—yes, establish the work of our hands (Psalms 90:17).

In everything you do for the kingdom, let God guide you and let his power work through you. Trust in the Lord with all your heart and lean not on your own understanding. With God's help, you will have a maximum impact on the kingdom. You must shine your light in this dark world. You could be the closest thing to a Bible that a person will meet. When you're out in the world, be the way Christ Jesus was on this earth. Exhibit love, joy, peace, patience, goodness, faithfulness, gentleness, and self-control. Live your life as an example so that when you're witnessing, nobody can accuse you of being a hypocrite or lukewarm.

As you grow in your spiritual walk with God, you must do your part to witness, give, offer wise counsel, and do overall good works. Remember, this life isn't about you and always getting what you desire. God said if we put him first, all the extra stuff will be added, if it is in his will. Remember, we are on Earth to complete a mission. God sent his Spirit to guide us. He will establish the work of our hands. We all have gifts, and in using them for God, he gets the glory. Do not become weary in doing right. Stand firm in the fight. Jesus himself faced much opposition from people. He was the stone the builders rejected. He endured it so we can, too. Especially since our opposition cannot compare to what he endured. Let your light shine before men so they can see the glory of God.

Let God Do a New Thing

Sometimes we can't see what God is doing, but that is where faith comes in. God is always in your corner. He has your best interest in mind, and he wants you to prosper. I loved when God opened the servant's eyes in 2 Kings 6:17 when he was afraid of the Arameans. The servant said, "Oh no! Lord, what shall we do?" After the Lord opened his eyes, he saw the hills full of horses and chariots of fire all around Elisha. Even if we can't physically see it, God has our back. He fights our battles. It is important that, as children of God, we keep the Word in our hearts. "I have hidden your word in my heart that I might not sin against you" (Psalms 119:11). How can your faith increase without studying God's Word? The Word is our guide. God has given us a book that has instructions on how to live a righteous life. Faith comes from hearing the message, and the message is heard through the Word about Christ (Romans 10:17).

Let God do the work on you, but you must fully surrender to him first. You must have faith in God and believe his Word. Exhibit the fruits of the Spirit, follow the beatitudes, fear God, and follow the commandments. Plant the seeds of righteousness and watch God bring forth the fruit. God will do a new thing in your life and in others for whom you intercede. "I have planted, Apollos watered, but God gave the increase" (1 Corinthians 3:6). God is the only one responsible for your increase. He is able. Plant the Word in your heart and watch the fruit flourish.

Leave the past in the past. If you continue the old, flesh-ly habits, you cannot move forward. Repent and leave the old ways alone. Forgive people who have wronged you. Put God first. It is not about what you want and how you feel. Where in the Bible does it say to be in your feelings? Put God's Word above all. Obedience is key! When you obey his Word, you are on a path to many blessings. You are ful-filling God's calling on your life. You become a powerful prayer warrior. Anything you ask will be given to you if it's in God's will. You will spiritually prosper, and your name will be in the Lamb's Book of Life.

Disobey, and you are stuck. You won't be able to grow. God only hears the prayers of the righteous, so if you dis-obey God continually, you will be cut off from him. We've all fallen short of the glory of God, but when you become a new creature, you don't continue your disobedience. If you sin, you repent, and then you no longer commit that sin. Your treasure is where your heart is. If you are still living in your fleshly past, there will be dangerous eternal conse-quences.

In Genesis 19, two angels of the Lord came to the city of Sodom to warn Lot and his family to get out because the city was about to be obliterated. From heaven, the Lord heard the victims' cries, so he sent the angels to destroy the city. Lot, with his wife and two daughters, were told to flee, not to look back, and to go to the mountains or else they would be swept away. Once the Lord rained down burning sulfur on Sodom and Gomorrah, destroying everything and every person in the city, Lot's wife looked back and turned into a pillar of salt.

Right now, you are gambling with life or death. Living in the past leads to death. Doing a new thing leads to life. Leave your own personal Sodom and Gomorrah and go and sin no more.

Let the Old You Die

Once we become a new creature, we still must fight our flesh daily. Just because we are saved doesn't mean our flesh won't try to take control. We must actively crucify our flesh every day. We must walk according to the Spirit. "For whoever wants to save their life will lose it, but whoever loses their life for my sake will find it." (Matthew 16:25). Surrender completely to the power of God. He will help you tame your tongue, love others, turn the other cheek, forgive, control your anger so it doesn't give birth to sin, and so on.

With a sincere heart, present your request to God. Put the old you to death and let the new creature take control. Lose your fleshly life to gain eternal life. Jesus is the way, the truth, and the life. "The one who believes in him will live even though they die; and whoever lives by believing in me will never die" (John 11:25-26). Faith in Christ means even after your earthly death, your soul never dies. You will have eternal life through Christ Jesus. You will see the glory of God. Let the old worldly version of you die and be buried, and let the new you be born. Just like Jesus told Lazarus to come out of the cave, tell that new creature to come out.

Limitless Faith

"Then Jesus said, 'Did I not tell you that if you believed, you would see the glory of God?'" (John 11:40).

As we know, Abraham's faith was credited to him as righteousness. He believed God's promise to make his family into a great nation and bring them into a land with milk and honey. By faith, Noah built an ark because he believed God when he said he would destroy everyone with a flood. Moses had faith he could lead the Israelites out of Egypt.

In just these few examples, these men had faith without proof. Abraham never lived to see his family become a great nation, but he had faith. Noah had never seen a flood, but he still built the ark. Moses didn't have great speech, but he still led the Israelites out of slavery and into the desert. The greater the faith, the more God can use you to accomplish amazing things.

In modern times, we are not even asked to do as much as they did. Moses had to lead thousands of his people out of the country. Noah took over 100 years to build an ark. If they could do all of that, surely we can have faith in God. We put our full hope into Jesus and the one who sent him, the Most High. When we put our full trust and faith in God, he shares his kingdom with us. Jesus has prepared a room for us (John 14:2). In every circumstance, give God glory and understand that it is a part of God's will.

No matter what the situation looks like, just have faith. He is the one in control. It is a part of a bigger plan God has for you. He needs to train and develop you as an ambassador for Christ. "You are all sons of God through faith in Christ Jesus, for all of you who were baptized into Christ have clothed yourselves with Christ" (Galatians 3:26-27). When we confessed with our mouths that Jesus Christ was Lord and believed in our hearts that he was raised from the dead, we were saved by faith. Now, during our walk with God, we must continue to have faith and trust God's will.

We know God is always in control. We show we love and trust God by obeying his commands and by not worrying or being anxious when certain situations occur. We've already surrendered to his will, so in our walk, we must remind ourselves to cast our cares onto him because he cares for us. Don't be like Peter, who almost fell into the water when Jesus asked him to walk towards him. Have faith that God will pull you through any trial because it not only builds strength and character but ultimately gives God glory when you survive it and testify to others about it. How could God ever display his glory if we just skated through life without trials? "Truly I tell you, if you have faith as small as a mustard seed, you can say to this mountain, 'Move from here to there'; and it will move. Nothing will be impossible for you" (Matthew 17:20).

Faith is very powerful. Just believing that things will be taken care of is the beginning of faith. Faith is the evidence of things unseen. All you need is the faith of a mustard seed.

Without checking your account, knowing your paycheck is deposited into your account on payday is proof you can have faith. We must have that same energy with God. Faith can do amazing things. Faith can heal the sick. Faith can get bills paid without knowing where the money will come from. Faith is getting laid off from a job but knowing you won't get evicted. Have faith, no matter what. Believe God will do what he says he will do. "Everything is possible for the one who believes" (Mark 9:23).

Lonely Singles

When being single gets tough, we can keep in mind that Jesus understands our pain. Jesus was not married. He had no children. Often, he would go off by himself and pray to God. He understands being isolated. When he was on the cross dying for our sins, he was separated from the Father. The disciples were not there. Peter denied him three times. Judas betrayed him for thirty pieces of silver. Jesus knew he was the only one who could pay for the sins of many. That was probably a very isolated headspace. He was the one and only Messiah, the only one in the world who could save us from our sins.

When Jesus was tempted in the desert after fasting for 40 days and 40 nights, he was alone. There are seasons in life where you, too, will be alone. There won't be groups of friends constantly checking on you every day. There won't be a boyfriend or spouse to spend time with or children calling your name. While you are in your single season, be content and patient. Meditate on God's Word and continually pray you don't fall into temptation. There is nothing you are going through that Jesus hasn't faced. "For we do not have a high priest who is unable to empathize with our weaknesses, but we have one who has been tempted in every way, just as we are, yet he did not sin" (Hebrews 4:15). We are never truly alone because God is always with us. "Have I not command-ed you? Be strong and courageous. Do not be frightened, and do not be dismayed, for the Lord your God is with you wherever you go" (Joshua 1:9).

Like Jesus, some of us are called to live this life single. If being single is your calling, then you have more time to dedicate to God. Married individuals have a responsibility to God but also to their spouse. Being single is a gift and Apostle Paul stated it is better to be without a spouse. There are fewer distractions and one can be fully devoted to pleasing God.

If you are lonely, you must get to the root of your loneliness. Simply getting a spouse is not the answer to the real issue. And you cannot expect God to send you a spouse if you are not ready. To get past the feeling of loneliness, you must talk to God and pray. Ask him to help you with being content. Spend time studying the Word, elevating your professional career, giving to your community, spending time with family, and so on. Make sure you are doing positive things that keep you busy. If you desire a spouse, and it is in his will for you to get married, he will not send that person until you show him you are content. Seek ye first the kingdom of God and all its righteousness, and all these things will be given to you as well.

Love

"Love is patient, love is kind. It does not envy, it does not boast, it is not proud" (1 Corinthians 13:4).

As Christ's ambassadors, we must always operate in love. We must love our neighbors and exhibit the fruit of the Spirit. We must be patient with our neighbor in forgiving trespasses, just as God is patient with us. How can you love others if you are coveting what they have? Bragging about material things or your net worth is not operating in love. "[Love] does not dishonor others, it is not self-seeking, it is not easily angered, it keeps no record of wrongs. Love does not delight in evil but rejoices with the truth" (v. 5, 6).

Love means respecting others and putting others above yourself. Be slow to anger and quick to forgive. And once you forgive, the past should be erased. Jesus said he removes our transgressions from us as far as the east is from the west. And we are supposed to imitate Christ. Love means not rejoicing when evil is being done. Love what God loves, and detest what God detests; only rejoice in the truth, for the truth sets everyone free.

Humble yourselves like Jesus did on this earth. Associate with those of low position. Do not repay others for what evil they have done. If we all paid for the wrongs we'd done, we would be in hell right now with no chance of salvation. Show the same grace to others the Father shows to us. Be generous and live at peace on this earth. "It always protects, always trusts, always hopes, always perseveres" (v. 7). Choose love. It never fails.

Meditate on his Word

"...But whose delight is in the law of the Lord, and who meditates on his law day and night. That person is like a tree planted by streams of water, which yields its fruit in season and whose leaf does not wither—whatever they do prospers" (Psalms 1: 2-3).

"I meditate on your precepts and consider your ways" (Psalms 119:15).

As children of God, we are in constant battle in our minds. Satan tempts us and presents ideas to us. If we live by the Spirit, we can defeat him. We can silence those negative thoughts. We don't let the flesh win. We are obedient to God's commands, and we love to obey. We constantly study his Word and apply it to our lives. When we align our ways with God's ways, our lives prosper. The Word was given to us to help us, not harm us. We can lead truly content lives knowing we're doing what's right in the eyes of God. There is peace in obedience.

Meditating on his Word and keeping it in your heart is profitable for witnessing, teaching, fighting the enemy, and rebuking. Keeping your mind on God means less time for Satan to creep in. A child of God who delights in his law will produce good spiritual fruit. Remember, you are what you consume. If you meditate on ratchetness and wickedness, you produce rotten fruit. Meditate on all things godly, and there will be a sweet aroma of good fruit.

Miracles from the Grave

In 2 Kings chapter 13, Jehoash is now King of Israel. He did evil in God's sight and never sought the Lord. Elisha was deathly ill, and Jehoash came to visit him. Elisha told him to shoot an arrow through the east window. This represented Israel's victory over Aram. Elisha then told him to strike the ground with arrows. Jehoash did this three times and stopped. Elisha said he should have struck the ground more times. The number of arrows struck to the around equaled the number of times Aram would be defeated. After Elisha died, they buried him.

One day, some Israelites were burying a dead man when Moabite raiders entered the country. The Israelite men threw the man's body into Elisha's tomb. When the man's body touched Elisha's bones, the man came back to life and stood on his feet. And just like Elisha had prophesied, Jehoash defeated Aram and recovered the Israelite towns. During the life of Elisha, he was able to raise a boy from the dead, make an ax head float to the top of the water, multiply oil in jars so the woman could pay her debts, help end a famine, make a poisonous stew edible again, multiply 20 loaves of bread to feed 100 men, help Naaman cleanse himself of leprosy, trap blinded Arameans, provide wise counsel to the king, help a woman get her land back, and prophesy in the name of the Lord. This is what strong faith and obedience can achieve.

Then, even after his death, his bones raised a dead man to life. Even after death, he still worked a miracle as God's vessel, like Jesus, who, after death and resurrection, still works miracles every day. Obedience and faith make God's servants unstoppable. We serve a faithful God who rewards our faithfulness.

New Creature

"I will give you a new heart, and I will put a new spirit in you. I will take out your stony, stubborn heart" (Ezekiel 36:26).

You have surrendered your life to Christ, and the old you is no more. You are a new creature doing a new thing. You are not defined by your past behavior. God said, "If my people who are called by my name shall humble themselves, and pray, and seek my face and turn from their wicked ways, then will I hear from heaven and will forgive their sin and will heal their land." God was waiting on you all along. He never leaves us; we are the ones who walk away from God.

The angels in heaven rejoice every time a sinner is saved. With God on your side, he gives you the power to fight the flesh. He can help you with whatever weakness you have. Now that you are saved, God hears your prayers. "The Lord is far from the wicked, but he hears the prayer of the righteous" (Proverbs 15:29). "And the fervent prayer of the righteous availeth much" (James 5:16). You no longer do what you want to do; you relinquish your will for God's will. You can only do what God allows you to do.

Living for God requires obedience and rejecting what the world deems acceptable. Be faithful to God because he is trustworthy, and he will bless you for your obedience and patience. Through Christ, we are equipped to handle what will come our way. We may be mocked and persecuted, but God made us warriors through him who paid for our sins. Must Christ carry his cross alone? We must bear our cross and walk with God. We were created to do good works and to be set apart from this world. We should not adopt the mindset of the world, because the Word says not to conform to the pattern of this world but to be transformed by the renewing of our minds. Finally, do not let Satan try to convince you that your old life was much more fun. That road leads to eternal death. Now that you are saved, do not go back to your old vomit.

You are on Satan's radar now. The adversary is determined to derail God's children, just like he tempted Eve in the Garden of Eden. He doesn't waste time with sinners because they are already rebelling against God. As soon as a sinner even thinks about repentance, the adversary is working overtime to discourage them from repenting and walking with God. He comes to steal, kill, and destroy. He wants you to indulge your flesh so you can backslide and be back with him.

In John chapter 8, Jesus explains who belongs to God and who belongs to the devil. If they believed in him, then they were his disciples. Of those who rejected him and wanted to kill him, he said that their father is the devil, a liar and murderer from the beginning. If they belonged to God, they would love Jesus. Those who rejected Christ and wanted him dead wanted to carry out their father's (devil's) desires.

One is either walking with the Lord or the enemy. There is no middle ground.

On Fire for the Lord

"Whoever believes in me, as Scripture has said, rivers of living water will flow from within them" (John 7:38).

Jesus Christ says that whoever is in him and he in them will bear the fruits of the Spirit, thus inheriting eternal life. It is our job to spread the gospel unabashedly to the world. As children of God, we should be on fire for Christ. "For I am not ashamed of the gospel, because it is the power of God that brings salvation to everyone who believes: first to the Jew, then to the Gentile" (Romans 1:16). We do not hold back witnessing because we care what others would think; we put God and his kingdom first. We think about how important their souls are and the consequences that will follow if they don't receive salvation. We know the wages of sin lead to death, so we know how crucial it is to spread the gospel. More importantly, to do this, we must be governed by the Holy Spirit, living not as unwise but as wise, making the most of every opportunity, because the days are evil. "Therefore, do not be foolish, but understand what the Lord's will is" (Ephesians 5:15-17).

Make sure your affairs are in order first so you can, in good conscience, witness and give your testimony. If you are stagnant for the kingdom, you must get serious about God. "'Wake up, sleeper, rise from the dead, and Christ will shine on you" (Ephesians 5:14). You need an awakening right now. And when you become on fire for God, his light will shine through you.

Overcoming

"Be strong and courageous. Do not be afraid or terrified because of them, for the Lord your God goes with you; he will never leave you nor forsake you" *(Deuteronomy 31:6).*

It's easy to feel alone in this world, but you are never alone with God. When you are walking with God, you have a relationship with the Father. He knows your heart. You never have to feel afraid with God on your side; who can be against you? No matter what situation you find yourself in, God is right there. We can't see him, but he is there. He said he won't leave us nor forsake us. Isn't that comforting?

In all situations, give thanks and let the Word of God comfort you. He is the problem fixer and miracle worker. He works in mysterious ways in his own time. Prayer is the believer's way of communicating with the Father. Ask, seek, knock. All we must do is pray in Jesus's name, and we will receive it if it is in God's will. Jesus is the way, the truth, and the life. No one comes to the Father except through him. Thank God for an intercessor like Jesus. He washed us clean and put us in right relationship with Father God.

Most importantly, have faith that God has the power to do what needs to be done. God can help you overcome any situation or circumstance. If you keep your mind focused on him, he will keep you in perfect peace. "Stand firm then, with the belt of truth buckled around your waist, with the breastplate of righteousness in place" (Ephesians 6:14). To overcome evil in this world, we need to be prepared. We have to *already* be ready. Putting on your breastplate of righteousness means arming yourself with the Word of God, constantly praying, fasting, and keeping a sober mind daily. It means that you treat your neighbor the way you would want to be treated.

The more Christlike you are, the more God can use you as his holy instrument. Every day you have to fight the fleshly part of you and live your life governed by the Holy Spirit. Remain on your guard and you will be ready for the adversary's schemes. We can't do it on our own. We need Christ's power to work within us. Christ died and was resurrected, thus defeating death. His sacrifice brought justification, so in him, we can become the righteousness of God (2 Corinthians 5:21).

When deciding, think to yourself, "What would Jesus do?" Let the Holy Spirit guide you in everything. When someone commits evil against you, do not return the same energy. That would make you no better than them. God doesn't need any help from you. Let God avenge you. Live in peace with everyone. Romans 12:18 says, "If it is possible, as far as it depends on you, live at peace with everyone." You cannot fight hate with hate; only love can overcome hatred and evil. God is love. Give to everyone, even to your enemy, and in doing so, heap burning coals onto their heads (Proverbs 25:22). Give them food and water, and God will reward you. We must be intercessors for our enemies the way Moses and Paul were. Pray for your enemies!

Peace

"Let the peace of Christ rule in your hearts, since as members of one body, you were called to peace. And be thankful" (Colossians 3:15).

The peace of God transcends all understanding. Let God give you rest. As members of the body of Christ, we are called to be peaceful with everyone around us. Be thankful that God chose you as his child. With God on your side, who can be against you? Clothe yourselves with the Holy Spirit and display all the fruits of the Spirit. Philippians 4:6 says, "Do not be anxious about anything, but in every situation, by prayer and petition, with thanksgiving, present your request to God." If God sacrificed his only begotten Son on the cross so that we may have life, then how much more would he give us if we just ask with faithful and obedient hearts? Show God that you believe he can handle any situation, no matter how difficult. Guard your heart and mind in Christ Jesus.

Pray for Others

In Philippians 1:2-7, Paul talks about how he prays for the believers in the Philippi church. He expresses his faith that Christ in them will continue to work through them: "He who began a good work in you will carry it on to completion until the day of Christ Jesus" (v. 6). This applies to us as believers today. We should pray more for others than we do for ourselves. We need to use our strengths to uplift other members of the body of Christ. We should pray that our brother or sister in Christ doesn't fall away but stands firm in the faith until Jesus comes back. Paul explains in verse 7 that whether he is in jail or preaching the gospel around the world, they share in God's grace with him. As Paul loves the body of Christ and wants them to have the same zeal for the kingdom, we need to have that same longing, the same hope.

We are to live the way Christ did on this earth. Christ put everyone else before himself. He was constantly teaching, helping, feeding, forgiving, sacrificing, and more. He loved God's children and wanted them to be strong in faith. Once you are a new creature, you do away with the old. You are now a new creature doing a new thing. Let the Word of God work in your Spirit. It will help you walk in righteousness. The Word of God does what God desires for it to do and will not come back to him void. It will achieve the purpose for which it was sent. Keep the Word in your heart, pray without ceasing, do good works, and sanctify yourself by the Word, which is truth.

Prayer Life

"And pray in the spirit on all occasions with all kinds of prayers and requests. With this in mind, be alert and always keep on praying for all the Lord's people" *(Ephesians 6:18).*

Go to God for everything: when things are great, when they are challenging, to give thanks to God, to repent, to intercede for others, etc. Keep the lines of communication open all day. Pray over your food. Pray that you drive safely. Let God know you are leaning on him for all your needs. Everything is in God's hands; "Rejoice always, pray continually, give thanks in all circumstances; for this is God's will for you in Christ Jesus" (1 Thessalonians 5:16-18).

No matter what is going on in your life, thank God at least for still being on this earth. God has given you life. Out of all the struggles that get thrown your way, at least you are still breathing. You have time to carry out God's will for your life. You can still get things right with the Lord. You can repent for past sins, do good works, and evangelize. Be grateful for the life God has given you. God gave us the blessing of being able to work a job and enjoy hobbies. All in all, this life is a blessing, and we only get one.

So, pray in all circumstances with the Spirit translating your groanings. The Lord hears your petitions. Stay on your guard and pray for the body of Christ. "Devote yourselves to prayer, being watchful and thankful" (Colossians 4:2). Devote means dedicate. Without distractions, dedicate your time to God and give thanks. Don't get lazy in your prayer life. Do not forget about how powerful prayer is. As children of God, we must pray constantly throughout the day. We deal with spiritual warfare, our own flesh, and, in general, worldly people. To stay grounded, we need God's protection. We need to thank God for his blessings.

We also need to pray for the body of Christ. "And pray in the Spirit with all kinds of prayers and requests. Be alert and always keep on praying for all the Lord's people" (Ephesians 6:18).

There are many examples in the Word of how effective prayer is. It has moved mountains, caused walls to fall, healed the sick, and effected many miracles. Prayer is our way of communicating with the Father and displaying our faith in him. Show God you believe he is able. If you continually pray and keep a strong faith, the enemy will be less likely to catch you off guard. We must watch and pray. Keep the full armor of God on. "This is the confidence we have in approaching God: that if we ask anything according to his will, he hears us. And if we know that he hears us — whatever we ask — we know we have what we asked of him" (1 John 5:14-15). A truly effective prayer is when one believes that if it is in God's will, they will receive whatever they have asked of him.

Profanity

"Out of the same mouth come praise and cursing. My brothers, this should not be. Can both fresh water and saltwater flow from the same spring?" (James 3:10-11).

Being holy and righteous is the goal of a child of God. How can one claim to walk with God if they are letting unholy words leave their lips? When one uses profane words, does that give an appearance of being filled with the Holy Spirit? Quite the exact opposite. You are operating with your flesh when you use your tongue to verbally assault someone made in the image of God. If someone claims to walk with God yet curses people out daily, they are exhibiting lukewarm behavior. You cannot be hot and cold at the same time. "I know your deeds, that you are neither cold nor hot. I wish you were either one or the other! So, because you are lukewarm—neither hot nor cold—I am about to spit you out of my mouth" (Revelation 3:15-16). We may stumble but we repent and ask God to help us in our weaknesses. You can't be holy and, at the same time, "yet does not keep a tight rein on his tongue" (James 1:26). Choose today whom you will serve, God or your flesh. James 1:22 says be ye doers of the word, and not hearers only, deceiving your own selves. It is not enough to just know the scripture; one must apply it to their lives. Your life and works must reflect

God's Word. James says that just knowing the Word and not doing what it says is like a man looking in the mirror and, after looking at himself, goes away and instantly forgets what he looks like. A man or woman who understands and does what the law says will be blessed. The person who follows Gods laws, looks after orphans, widows, the unfortunate, and is not worldly — this is what the Father finds pure and faultless.

Purpose

"Let us hear the conclusion of the whole matter: fear God and keep his commandments, for this is the whole duty of man" (Ecclesiastes 12:13).

American society would have you believe everyone should have a white-picket-fence lifestyle. You get good grades in K-12, go to college, get a career, get married, and have a nuclear family. Now there is nothing wrong with any of this, but life is more than a degree and a job. For children of God, there is a much greater purpose on this earth. Humans were created to worship God. After a third of the angels rebelled against God, he made man after his own image. We were to live in the Garden of Eden, enjoy paradise, eat fruit, never age, and not have to work.

That was destroyed once Adam disobeyed God by eating the forbidden fruit. That created a domino effect and, fast forward to today, most of us have forgotten and/or do not know why we are supposed to be on this earth. Some think they are here only to find a date. Some think they are here only to gain power and have control of a big corporation. All of us were born with this void inside of our soul. God meant for us to fill that void with him. We were created to have a relationship with our Father. Our purpose is to revere God and keep his commandments.

We are not here to do what we want to do. That's what

your flesh convinces you to think and the mindset the enemy strongly encourages you to have. Your flesh naturally wants to rebel. Humans think they have it all figured out. We all try to play the role of God and think we have control. We have no control. Our life is nothing but a passing vapor. God is the one in control, and the enemy is the god ruling this world. If you are not doing what God called you to do, you are advancing the adversary's agenda.

It is not enough to just be a "good person." Being a good person doesn't equate to walking with God. Apostle Paul wrote that not one of us is good because we were all born into sin. Jesus Christ was the only person born on this earth who was truly good because he never sinned. God's will for us is to surrender to him, repent of our sins, take up our cross, obey his commands, and advance the gospel. He wants all the lost sheep to return to the shepherd.

Remember, your purpose isn't about superficial things you see in Hollywood movies or on Instagram. Understand that you have a greater mission in Christ Jesus. It's not about self-interest. It's about the two greatest commandments: 1) Love the Lord your God with all your heart and with all your soul and with all your mind, and 2) love your neighbor as yourself.

Remain Faithful

When Elisha went to Shunem, a woman fed him bread and took great care of him. He then asked her what he could do for her. She asked for a child. He told her she would be nursing a babe at that time the next year. Of course, it came to pass.

Years later, the child fell sick. The woman saddled a donkey and went to Elisha. Elisha went to the woman's house and saw the child was dead. He stretched himself over the child and prayed. The child was not alive. Elisha left the house, returned, and stretched himself onto the child again. The child sneezed seven times and opened his eyes.

When God is working the blessing, don't stop praying and having faith he will deliver. "The first time Elisha stretched out on him; the flesh of the child waxed warm" (2 Kings 4:34). The first time we pray for something, there might not be an immediate result, but don't lose faith. We need an even stronger faith to believe God will eventually deliver. And when he delivers, be prepared to give God the glory.

The Shunamite woman had faith when she sought Elisha. She believed God would heal her son through Elisha. There are situations only God can fix. No matter how dire things get, we can search for the solution in God. Let his will be done. In the Shunamite's case, God brought back her son for his glory.

Sacrifice

"My Father, if it is not possible for this cup to be taken away unless I drink it, may your will be done" (Matthew 26:42).

A friend is one who will lay their life down for you. Jesus is the greatest friend in all human history. He laid down his life while we were yet sinners so we could be in right relationship with God. Because of Jesus' sacrifice, eternal life is possible through faith. He endured taunts, insults, drinking of bile, nails in his hands and feet, flogging, etc., all for us, knowing he never deserved it. He was without sin, yet he took on sin and defeated death. He endured temptation from the adversary and remained strong.

He had human emotions like us. He wept when Lazarus died. In verse 37, he was full of sorrow when he went to Gethsemane with the disciples and prayed to the Father. He knew he was about to be crucified, and it was troubling him. Imagine knowing you are about to be painfully persecuted. Thank God he sent his only begotten Son. We don't have to endure the cross, but we must sacrifice for God. This life is not about having fun and doing what we want. It's about letting God's will be done. As sorrowful as Jesus was, he said, "If this can't be taken away, Father let YOUR will be done." We must have the same energy. What are you willing to sacrifice for God?

Satan has Already Lost

Satan attacks God's children. We know this through studying the Word. In Genesis 3, the serpent deceived Eve into eating the fruit, and the disobedience caused sin to come into the world. Therefore, there was enmity between mankind and God. Thus, we were all born into sin. When Jesus died on the cross for our sins, he defeated death. And our faith in Jesus gives us eternal life, and now we are in right relationship with God. There is no longer enmity between us (children of God) and the Father.

As God's children, we have the power through Christ to fight the enemy. We pray, fast, and use the Word to dispute Satan's lies. He comes to steal, kill, and destroy. God has the authority and won't let you be tempted beyond what you can bear. He will provide a way out. God knew from the beginning that Jesus would have the victory. No weapon formed against you shall prosper. But when you are tested, count it joy, because that means you are a true child of God.

Satan doesn't waste time on *his* children because they are already carrying out his will. While they indulge their flesh, they are on their way to hell with Satan. This is Satan's agenda. Rejoice in your sufferings, because you must be doing something right. This Scripture comes to mind in Job 1:8, "'Have you considered my servant Job? There is no one on earth like him; he is blameless and upright, a man who fears God and shuns evil.'" So, count it joy if God says this about you.

The adversary must get permission from God to test you. "Very well, then, everything he has is in your power, but on the man himself do not lay a finger" (v. 12). Cast your cares onto God, because he cares for you." And the God of all grace, who called you to his eternal glory in Christ, after you suffered a little while, will himself restore you and make you strong, firm, and steadfast" (1 Peter 5:10).

We know the enemy's time is short, so he is working overtime and double time. But remember that you have the victory through Christ. God will never forsake you. He will sustain you.

Spiritual Growth

Philippians 1:9-11 discusses how constantly studying the Word and growing in godliness has benefits. As you spiritually grow, you will have more discernment about God's will for your life. You will feel convicted about certain things that you should not be doing. You will hear God more clearly. God wants us to get closer to him. He wants us to have an intimate relationship with him. That is what we were created for, to have a relationship with him and to worship him.

At some point, we must get off the Similac milk and graduate to solid food. God is good, and he approves of all things praiseworthy, things that glorify his name. His will for us includes advancing the gospel, putting on the full armor of God, and standing firm until Jesus' return. We cannot give up; rather, we press on to receive our inheritance. If we choose to walk with him, we acknowledge that the journey is never easy. Our goal is not to remain stagnant, but to grow with God. Doing that requires more trials and tribulations, for this builds strength, character, and perseverance.

Let God pour out his Spirit on you. Thirst and hunger for his righteousness and prepare for an overflow of blessings. Continue to carry out his will, and he will direct your path. "We must pay the most careful attention, therefore, to what we have heard, so that we do not drift away" (Hebrews 2:1).

This verse encourages us to keep ourselves immersed

in the Word of God so we don't get dragged back into the world. We need to be constantly studying, praising, listening to worship music, and so on, to keep our mind on all things holy. We also must lift up the body of Christ and hold each other accountable. "But encourage one another daily, as long as it is called 'Today', so that none of you may be hardened by sin's deceitfulness" (Hebrews 3:13). Don't let your brother or sister in Christ become hardened to God's Word. Love what the Lord loves and hate what he hates. Draw near to righteousness and flee from sin. One cannot remain a babe in Christ forever. When it comes to our spiritual journey, you must eventually graduate from kindergarten and then move on to earn a high school diploma, then a college degree, and so on.

Spiritual Warfare

"Be on your guard; stand firm in the faith; be men of courage; be strong. Do everything in love" (1 Corinthians 16:13-14)

At all times, we must be very aware and vigilant because we do not fight against flesh; rather, we battle against spirits, for it is a spiritual war. Our mission includes standing our ground against unbelievers, persecutors, and hypocrites, and declaring the Word of God. We are the light of the world, so we must keep the lamps lit and on a stand for the world to see. As Christ ambassadors, we are supposed to set the example.

No matter what you come up against, have courage. "For the Lord your God is the one who goes with you to fight for you against your enemies to give you victory" (Deuteronomy 20:4). We can give it to God and rely on him, because he is trustworthy and faithful in his unfailing love. Remain strong and don't give in to your weaknesses.

Remember that bad company corrupts good character. Be very mindful of who you have in your company. Either you will draw them to your light, or you will be drawn to their darkness. Walk with God completely and use your sword. He will direct your path. "In addition to all this, take up the shield of faith, with which you can extinguish all the flaming arrows of the evil one" (Ephesians 6:16). You need a strong faith to come up against the enemy; we are fighting against principalities, dark forces, and the rulers of this world. Faith is the key for protection. It's just like the movie *The Matrix*. Within the matrix, there were evil creatures that wanted to harm everyone, but people could not see them. They were blinded. It is a lot like reality. We are in a spiritual war that worldly people cannot see. Second Corinthians 4:4 says, "The god of this age has blinded the minds of unbelievers, so that they cannot see the light of the gospel that displays the glory of Christ, who is the image of God." The adversary is always on his job.

Faith can accomplish many things. The faith of a mustard seed can move mountains. That lets you know how powerful it is. Faith comes from hearing the Word concerning Christ (Romans 10:17). And when that faith leads to deliverance from the enemy, then you have your testimony. Your testimony will strengthen someone else's faith.

"Take the helmet of salvation and the sword of the Spirit, which is the word of God" (Ephesians 6:17). Take the confidence that you have in God's grace when you go into battle. Do not listen to the enemy's lies about a lack of salvation. He wants you to doubt your salvation. Protect your mind with Christ, so you will not have itching ears that easily give way to false doctrine, ideologies, quarrels about genealogies, etc. Pray to God he gives you a sound mind. The mind is what Satan often tries to attack. Use the Word of God to fight his antics. When he tries to spout lies about you, tell him you are fearfully and wonderfully made. When you feel weary, tell him no weapon formed against you shall prosper. Have faith in God's power, and he will keep you in your right mind.

For future battles to come, it is important to be righteous and not worldly. "Rather clothe yourselves with the Lord Jesus Christ, and do not think about how to gratify the desires of the flesh" (Romans 13:14). You cannot fight the flesh on your own. You need the power of Christ, which is only given to those who obey and love him. The only way to show you love God is to follow his ways, study to show thyself approved, abide in good works, give thanks in all circumstances, and live your life governed by the Holy Spirit.

We should want to thank Christ as much as possible because he saved us from eternal damnation. We were in danger of the wrath of God, but Jesus paid the price for our sin. We were adopted into the kingdom as co-heirs with Christ. We can do all things through him who strengthens us. We are in the end game now, and Jesus is on his way back. Nobody knows the day or hour we will die, so do not let one day go to waste. Tomorrow is not promised. Obey God's commands and, most importantly, seek ye first the kingdom of God and all its righteousness.

Stand Firm

"Let us not become weary in doing good, for at the proper time we will reap a harvest if we do not give up" (Galatians 6:9).

Sometimes, we become impatient and weary in doing the right thing. We want to reap our blessings immediately. One must always remember that God has perfect timing. We must continue to serve God and do good works. We must put our minds on things above instead of earthly things. If we continue to hold fast to God's commands and decrees, we will be rewarded in heaven. We must fulfill our purpose and do good to all people, not just the ones who are good to us.

God wants to know what is truly in our hearts. Our faith will be tested at times. Remember that the faith of a mustard seed can move mountains. Luke 18:1 says we should pray and never give up. There is a reason for every season. Every chapter has its purpose. God is always at work in our lives. He hears the prayers of the righteous. He is a just and good God. Meanwhile, dwell on all the times God has delivered you, healed you, and spared your life. Give God thanks for what he has already done. Reflect on how the Israelites forgot how good God was to them (Psalms 106:7-18).

James 1:14 says, "But each person is tempted when they are dragged away by their own evil desire and enticed." If we give in to our own lust and desires and forget God's promises, there will be consequences. Obey God, remember the miracles he had already displayed, and give thanks. Be patient for your blessings. Delays don't mean God's purpose isn't being fulfilled. God is always with us. God is forever faithful to those who love him.

Status of your Soul

"For we must all appear before the judgment seat of Christ, so that each of us may receive what is due us for the things done while in the body, whether good or bad" (2 Corinthians 5:10).

There is only God and the devil. Heaven or hell. Even if a person does not believe that premise is true, nobody has come back from the dead to confirm or deny that truth. For those of us who believe the Bible is the infallible word of truth, we believe that we have a Creator we answer to. In these last days, it is important to know where we all stand in relation to heaven and hell.

There are a few categories that broadly cover billions of people. Of course, there are people who have a relationship with God. "Yet to all who did receive him, to those who believed in his name, he gave the right to become children of God—children born not of natural descent, nor of human decision or a husband's will, but born of God" (John 1:12-13). Then, there are people who go to church but also do what they want to do. They have one foot in and one foot out; this is called *lukewarm*. "So, because you are lukewarm, and neither hot nor cold, I will spit you out of my mouth" (Revelation 3:16). Matthew 5:13 says, "You are the salt of the earth. But if the salt loses its saltiness, how can it be made salty again? It is no longer good for anything, except to be thrown out and trampled underfoot." When you are spiritually lukewarm, God cannot use salt that has lost its saltiness. You will be thrown into the same lake of fire that unbelievers will be thrown into if you do not repent and sin no more.

Then there are hypocrites who ostentatiously proclaim how sanctified they are, yet in their hearts, they are evil. "He replied, 'Isaiah was right when he prophesied about you hypocrites; as it is written: "These people honor me with their lips, but their hearts are far from me"'" (Mark 7:6).

There are unbelievers, who don't believe in God at all. "Whoever believes in him is not condemned, but whoever does not believe stands condemned already because they have not believed in the name of God's one and only Son" (John 3:18).

Then there are people who believe what they are doing is right. They truly are convinced their god is the one true God. In John 14:6, Jesus answered, "I am the way and the truth and the life. No one comes to the Father except through me." Jesus is the only way to salvation. He is the gateway to heaven. There is NO other way.

People also believe that their way of life or traditions are acceptable and right. This includes people who constantly make statements like, "I grew up in church." A relationship with God is not about a church building. And God doesn't care about what you did in the past. It's about what you are doing right now. The past is the past. There are no justifications or loopholes for the daily sin people decide to indulge in. They went to church as a child, and they try to live off that for the rest of their lives; meanwhile, they do everything that God detests. "There is a way that appears to be right, but in the end, it leads to death" (Proverbs 14:12).

God acknowledges that many people would try to find their own way, but ultimately, it leads to death. There are eternal consequences when a person makes up their own religion. Humans have made everything a religion. There's an Instagram religion, a yoga religion, a dating app religion, a political religion, and more. The Oxford Dictionary defines religion as a pursuit or interest to which someone ascribes supreme importance. Isaiah 53:6 says, "We all, like sheep, have gone astray, each of us has turned to our own way; and the LORD has laid on him the iniquity of us all."

No matter which category you fall under, understand that God has given you a choice. We are not robots forced to worship him. But everyone should know the truth. There are eternal consequences based on the most important decision in your life. I hope that everyone turns away from sin to have a relationship with God and not make up their own rules so they can still do what they want to do, but be a true servant of Christ, ready to give up their flesh so they may have eternal life. "If it is hard for the righteous to be saved, what will become of the ungodly and the sinner?" (1 Peter 4:18-19). God says that it will be difficult for even the righteous to make it into heaven, so imagine what is to come for the lukewarm, hypocrites, unbelievers, and people who worship false gods?

Stay on your Guard

"Be alert and of sober mind. Your enemy, the devil, prowls around like a roaring lion looking for someone to devour. Resist him, standing firm in the faith, because you know that the family of believers throughout the world is undergoing the same kind of sufferings" (1 Peter 5:8-9).

As a child of God, we are not supposed to be drunk, high, or under any influence of a toxic substance that dangerously affects our minds. If you become intoxicated, you need to sober up and repent immediately with a sincere heart. You are indulging in the flesh. "The acts of the flesh are obvious: sexual immorality, impurity and debauchery; idolatry and witchcraft; hatred, discord, jealousy, fits of rage, selfish ambition, dissensions, factions and envy; drunkenness, orgies, and the like. I warn you, as I did before, that those who live like this will not inherit the kingdom of God" (Galatians 5:19-21).

If you had a backslidden or lukewarm moment, then it's possible to repent. As long as we have breath in our bodies, we can repent, but there is no excuse to commit the same sin repeatedly. We must choose who we are serving. Being intoxicated is what the enemy wants you to be. As long as you're not in your right mind, you are not serving God. The enemy wants everyone distracted so that they will be outside of the will of God. And thus, they will be judged and thrown into the lake of fire.

As children of God, we must be an example to backsliders, hypocrites, and people of various religions. Our lives and decisions reflect our Father. We are Christ's ambassadors, so we must abide by the Word. Stay on your guard. We are in the last and evil days, so God needs his warriors to suit up with the full armor of God. Satan is always on his job, so as God's children, we must be just as proactive. You are not the only ones who are fighting battles. The whole body of Christ is fighting with their swords as well. A strong faith is needed in these end times.

Suffering

"I consider that our present sufferings are not worth comparing with the glory that will be revealed in us" *(Romans 8:18).*

No matter what we go through in life, those sufferings are not worth comparing to the glory that is to come. The trials and tribulations we face are necessary, and we endure them in this life by having hope of the glory that will be revealed in us. Colossians 3:2 says, "Set your affection on things above, not on things on this earth." We wait in eager expectation for the sons of God to be revealed above (Romans 8:19). When we gave our lives to Christ and confessed that Jesus died on the cross for our sins, we became new creatures. That did not mean we would stop having trials. It meant we were freed from the bondage of sin and adopted into the kingdom. We can rejoice in the fact that we are liberated. We now have God on our side to give us strength and fight our battles. Take comfort that there is something greater than mortal existence on earth.

Tell the Storm About Your God

In Matthew 8, when the disciples entered the boat and a storm was appearing, they went to wake up Jesus. Apparently, the storm worried them. "Lord, save us, we're going to drown!" (v. 25). Before Jesus rebuked the winds, he told them, "You of little faith, why are you so afraid?" (v. 26). Even though they had the Lord in the boat with them, they still doubted his power, thinking they would drown. They needed a stronger faith. If they had a strong faith, they wouldn't have awakened him.

Today, we also have Jesus in the boat with us and we still worry when a storm comes. Our storm could be a past-due bill, a divorce, a wayward child, a difficult boss, etc. The important thing is there is no storm Jesus cannot handle. We must let him know we trust him during a storm. Just like in the scripture, Jesus calmed the storm, and he will do it for you, too.

"Then he got up and rebuked the winds and the waves, and it was completely calm" (v. 26). Jesus will rebuke your storm. And it is all for God's glory. "Even the winds and the waves obey him! (v. 27). He has the power and authority overall. Trust in him and have faith.

The Called

"And we know that in all things God works for the good of those who love him, who have been called according to his purpose" (Romans 8:28).

God chose you. "You did not choose me, but I chose you and appointed you so that you might go and bear fruit—fruit that will last—and so that whatever you ask in my name the Father will give you" (John 15:16). You are called according to his purpose. He knew in the beginning who would choose him and who would not choose him. The ones who he knew would put him first and accept Christ are the called.

Everything that happens in life is a part of a bigger plan. Your promotion comes from God. Power does not come from man. We cannot control anything. God is always in control and the power belongs to him. He has the power to bless you with a family, a new job, a clean bill of health, that nonprofit you've been thinking about starting, or the inspiration to write a new book. The sky is the limit with God when you are called and, hopefully, accept that calling. When you seek ye first the kingdom of God and all his righteousness, all these things will be given to you as well.

When it comes to the Lord's children, he will provide all you ask according to his will. Ask and you shall receive, seek and you will find. Knock and the door will be opened.

God called you. You were predestined. You didn't choose him, he chose you. "Before I formed thee in thy belly, I knew thee; and before thou camest forth out of the womb I sanctified thee, and I ordained thee a prophet unto the nations" (Jeremiah 1:5, KJV). Before you even knew who you were, God knew you and called you. You were born into this generation for a reason. He knew he would need you to plant seeds of righteousness in this world — to spread the good news.

We are in a time where everything wrong is considered right according to society. You should use your gifts to build up the kingdom and give God all the glory. We give the glory unto his name, not onto ourselves. Know who you are in Christ and walk in your divine purpose. You are no longer in bondage to sin, rather you are now a slave to righteousness. "As a prisoner for the Lord, then I urge you to live a life worthy of the calling you have received" (Ephesians 4:1).

The Enemy's Battle Plan

"The God of peace will soon crush Satan under your feet" (Romans 16:20).

Every negative thought, feeling, or dream can come from the adversary. It's only you, God, and the enemy. God is good, so he only encourages you to be good. If he gives you a dream, it is something that will help you in your walk with him. But anything that is opposite of godly and encourages you to go against God, it is from the father of lies. He encourages every negative thought and feeling. Being in one's feelings never ends well. It has led people to kill, commit adultery, and be envious. These are all things God detests. God never told you to be in your feelings; he told you to use wisdom. He never said to have feelings about the actions of others, care about their appearance, or be upset about someone getting a promotion over you.

The enemy always encourages pride, envy, and wrath. However, he can't force you to do anything. He only takes your own desires, presents ideas, and encourages you to take them further so they give birth to sin. While the god of this world rules it, as children of God we know we must suit up in the full armor of God. We must rebuke the devil in Jesus's name. Jesus was also tested, and he had scripture to fight the enemy. But we know God works for the good of those who love him and are called according to his purpose.

God goes out and fights for us.

We know by the Word that God will throw Satan in the lake of fire where he can't lie, steal, kill, or destroy any longer. Like Michael the archangel said to the adversary, "the Lord rebuke you." To be prepared for battle, we must build ourselves up in the faith, constantly praying in the Holy Spirit. Have faith that God will make the enemy a footstool for your feet. David said, "You prepare a table from me in the presence of my enemies. You anoint my head with oil, my cup overflows" (Psalm 23:5). God loves you and he has the authority to cut off all evildoers.

The Enemy's Deception

We were all born into sin after the first trespass in the Garden of Eden. After Adam and Eve ate the fruit and disobeyed God, sin came into the world. When Jesus died for our sins, he became the new Adam. The sacrifice was greater than the trespass. When we confess with our mouths that Jesus Christ is Lord and believe God resurrected him, we are saved. We are co-heirs with Christ.

But it doesn't stop there. The Word tells us we are to follow the commandments, display the fruit of the Spirit, adhere to the beatitudes, pray, worship, study, govern ourselves according to the Spirit, and overall be doers of the Word. Do not believe the worldly lie, "once saved, always saved." This is simply not true. The Word discusses how the cowardly, the unbelieving, the vile, the murderers, the sexually immoral, those who practice magic, idolaters, and all liars will be consigned to the fiery lake of burning sulfur (Revelation 21:8). Once you are saved, you cannot do what you want.

The world wants you to think that a person will go to heaven if they just go to church. Some people believe that those who are promiscuous and those who use profanity, as well as liars, prostitutes, drug users, drunkards, homosexuals, racists, abusers, etc. are all worthy of eternal paradise. They think God accepts any and everything. This is the trick of the enemy. The god of this world has blinded their eyes.

Satan wants people to believe that they can live however they want to because he knows the truth. He knows the Word better than most people who claim to be "Christians." Satan knows that if they are outside of the will of God, they will die in their sins and be in hell with him, so he wants everyone to continue to be distracted and think "I'm a good person, so I'll go to heaven." God has given us a manual for how to live on this earth, and it is his Word. Do not be deceived. Everything that we need is already in the Bible.

The Power of Prayer

"And she made a vow, saying, 'Lord almighty, if you will only look on your servant's misery and remember me, and not forget your servant but give her a son. Then I will give him to the Lord for all the days of his life, and no razor will ever be used on his head'" (1 Samuel 1:11).

Hannah desperately wanted a son, and being without a child brought her much sorrow. She was also being tormented by her husband's other wife, who often taunted her about being barren. But Hannah was a praying woman with a sincere heart. She also had to have faith that almighty God would grant her petition. Even more so, she offered her future son back to God. All good things come from the Lord. She had faith that God would bless her, so she wanted to show how thankful she was by giving her son to God.

When God blesses us, we must return a portion back to him with thanksgiving. We are not giving anything away; we are only returning what God has given to us. Our first thought should be to pray about any and everything. When you comfort yourself with the Word of God and continually pray, you can rest in the peace of God. Nobody ever said there wouldn't be struggles or hills to climb, but through prayer, God will give you peace to deal with any situation. Look at everything from God's perspective. Stay armed up and with your feet fitted with the readiness that comes from the gospel of peace (Ephesians 6:15). With a strong faith, we have peace through our Lord Jesus Christ (Romans 5:1). Jesus has already overcome the world.

The Special Coin that is Now Found

You are special. You are important. You matter. God loves and values you. In Luke 15:8-9, Jesus tells a parable about a woman who had ten coins but lost one. She lit her lamp and swept the house looking for it. When she found it, she and her neighbors rejoiced over finding the one lost coin. "In the same way, I tell you, there is rejoicing in the presence of the angels of God over one sinner who repents" (v. 10).

God doesn't want any of us to perish, and we must thank God for all the times he spared our lives while we were still in sin. The Shepherd cares about the sheep who go astray. It was God who protected you, nudged you with your conscience, and worked through others to get his lost sheep back. That shows how much you matter to God. When you turned away from your wicked ways and submitted to God completely, there was a celebration in heaven.

Every time you feel insignificant, just think about the parable of the lost coin. You are now found. You are loved and valued by God. He wants you to prosper spiritually. Don't focus on the adversary's lies. "Whatever is admirable, if anything is excellent or praiseworthy, think about such things" (Philippians 4:8). Meditate on God's Word and keep your mind on him. He will keep you in perfect peace.

Toxic Culture

"Do not conform to the pattern of this world but be transformed by the renewing of your mind. Then you will be able to test and approve what God's will is — his good, pleasing and perfect will" (Romans 12:2).

The modern-day American society is filled with feminism, social movements, pride parades, political correctness, and wars against political parties. Everyone wants to put a person in a box. They create new categories and identifiers every week. Everyone just wants to feel like they belong. Everyone just wants to be loved.

We live in a world where just stating that you stand by the infallible Word of God is hate speech. If you don't conform to their ideologies, you are being intolerant. Using the wrong pronouns means you are being hateful. Agreeing that people shouldn't create songs and videos that disrespect women and depict them in disparaging ways may be an unpopular opinion nowadays. Believing that you can't put your trust in man (Psalm 146:3) or in any political affiliations to the point of making them idols is also an unpopular stance. Jesus told us to just pay our taxes. Render unto Caesar what is due. "Then Jesus said to them, "Give back to Caesar what is Caesar's and to God what is God's" (Mark 12:17).

Don't get caught up in worldly quarrels. It is all a distraction of the enemy. We should focus on spreading the gospel to all nations. We are called to be fishers of men. When you are filled with the Holy Spirit, of course your mindset won't align with the world. The Spirit and the flesh are in conflict. You are using a biblical framework, the Word of God. Everyone else has come up with their own belief system, but remember, there is a way that seems right to man, but in the end, it leads to death (Proverbs 16:25). Our Lord Jesus Christ set a great example of how to live life. Do not conform to the patterns of this world, for it will all pass away. Stand firm in the faith and ignore worldly distractions. Anything that does not glorify Christ is a waste of time.

Transformation

God loves using the most unlikely people for his divine purpose. No matter your past, you can accomplish great things. God chose you. You were predestined by God. The greatest figures in the Bible were not Hollywood types. They didn't have the greatest looks or the best reputation, but God still chose them. "The LORD doesn't see things the way you see them. People judge by outward appearance, but the LORD looks at the heart" (1 Samuel 16:7).

Moses was insecure about his speech, yet God chose him to lead the Israelites out of Egypt. Samuel overlooked David among Jesse's sons because he wasn't the tallest or burliest. He was just a young, ruddy boy. As young as he was, David defeated the Philistine Goliath.

God loves using the unlikeliest people to fulfill his holy purposes. In the New Testament, Saul had Christians arrested. "Saul was still breathing out murderous threats against the Lord's disciples" (Acts 9:1). But in Damascus, Jesus came to him and asked him, "Why are you persecuting me?" He then gave him instructions. Saul was blind for three days. Meanwhile, the Lord told the disciple Ananias that Saul was his chosen instrument to proclaim his name to the Gentiles and Israel. Ananias then opened Saul's eyes, and he was filled with the Holy Spirit. He was baptized and instantly went to preaching that Jesus was the Messiah.

No matter whether you've been walking with God for

three days or thirty years, God can use you as his chosen instrument. Saul became Paul and became one of the greatest apostles. Let God transform you.

Trials

"For our light and momentary troubles are achieving for us an eternal glory that far outweighs them all" (2 *Corinthians 4:17*).

The struggles we experience on Earth are just momentary and build strength and character. It is all leading to a better place in the future. They can't compare to the glory you will experience one day: a place eternal, with no sadness or troubles. "So, we fix our eyes not on what is seen but on what is unseen" (v. 18). We should keep our minds on heavenly things above, not the things we experience on earth. "For what is seen is temporary, but what is unseen is eternal" (v. 18) The heavenly dwelling we long for is forever. What we can physically see is only here for a short time.

Jesus Christ gave his life as a deposit for us. This deposit guarantees what is to come if we believe in him, love him, and do God's work. Live by faith, not by sight. God can do his best work on us when we go through trials and tribulations. "For when I am weak, then I am strong" (2 Corinthians 12:10). Through illness, isolation, being single, wanting a promotion on the job, or financial struggles, God is still working on you. In this season, be more prayerful, stay focused, and continue to give thanks. God has a plan for you to prosper and have a future.

There was a man named Job in the Old Testament who

knew about trial and tribulation. He lost everything he had. Job was a very wealthy man with a wife and kids. One day, his flock and all his children were taken away from him. His wife started nagging him and telling him to curse God. There were sores all over his body. His friends kept accusing him of being unrighteous and deserving of everything that happened to him. But in Job 2:10, he asked, "Shall we accept good from God, and not trouble?"

Nobody ever said this life would be easy or that it should be. If Jesus died on the cross after being flogged, tortured, mocked, and betrayed, is he supposed to carry his cross alone? We all have a burden to bear. What type of person would we be if we never had trials? We would be spoiled, entitled brats with no regard for anyone but ourselves. Trials and tribulations make us stronger and more selfless. Have faith that God will give you the strength to endure it. He can deliver you from whatever situation you are in.

Unashamed of the Gospel

"Whatever happens, conduct yourselves in a manner worthy of the gospel of Christ. Then, whether I come and see you or only hear about you in my absence, I will know that you stand firm in the one Spirit, striving together as one for the faith of the gospel without being frightened in any way by those who oppose you. This is a sign to them that they will be destroyed, but that you will be saved—and that by God. For it has been granted to you on behalf of Christ not only to believe in him but also to suffer for him, since you are going through the same struggle you saw I had, and now hear that I still have" (Philippians 1:27-30).

In all matters, behave yourselves as Christ's ambassadors. Be examples of obedient children of God. Paul tells the church in Philippi that when he hears about them, he wants it to be positive. He wants to know they are standing firm in the faith. They need to spread the gospel unabashedly, even when adversaries come against them. Remember, the one in you is greater than the one in the world. Do not back down, because God gives you the strength to press on when scoffers are on the attack. By this, they will know that God is on your side. You will have eternal life through his grace. We must count it joy that we suffer like Paul did. For if we share in the sufferings of Jesus Christ, we will one day share in his glory in eternal paradise. We have faith because Christ died for us while we were yet sinners. So, rejoice in your momentary struggles, and stand firm in the faith.

Validation

"Am I now trying to win the approval of men, or of God?" (Galatians 1:10).

How easy it is to be swayed by the desire for human validation. Yet, we forget God's perfect and pleasing will. His approval should be what we seek. Obeying God's commands and not wanting to offend God should be the only concern. The apostle Paul said if he was trying to please man, he would not be a servant of Christ. One cannot both serve man and God. "Either you will hate the one and love the other, or you will be devoted to the one and despise the other" (Matthew 6:24). One cannot abide by worldly standards and serve God at the same time. Either you lose your life to follow Christ whilst gaining eternal life or gain the world and lose your soul. Serve God or the god of this world.

We must have faith to please God, spread the good news, do good works, and bear our cross. Paul also says to live by the Spirit, and you will not gratify the desires of the sinful nature. Ask the Lord to fill you with the Holy Spirit, and you will not desire to commit sinful acts. The Spirit contradicts the flesh. Both cannot coexist. Letting yourself be governed by the Spirit means you won't do what comes naturally to you. It's natural to indulge the flesh because we are all born into sin. It is human nature to rebel against God. For those who have accepted Christ into their hearts and walk with God, we have crucified our past sinful desires.

Paul states that we should not tire of doing good because if we continue to please the Spirit and not give up, we will have eternal life. Pleasing the world leads to the wide path of destruction.

The wages of sin are death. The world loves to validate sinful behavior. Therefore, if one who claims to be a follower of Christ yet secretly desires world validation, then they are a hypocrite. Must Jesus carry the cross alone? The world hated Jesus first. If you belonged to the world, it would love you as its own.

Stop desiring favorable opinions from sinners. Your goal should be spreading the gospel, not wanting the world's approval.

Waiting on Blessings

Don't be impatient and go outside of God's will to force things to happen. When it is from God, it will only come when you are ready. Stop focusing on when the blessing will come. Focus on ensuring you are ready. You don't want to accept what the adversary sends because it will throw you off course onto a dangerous path that will lead you away from God. God wouldn't send you something that would cause you to walk away from him. We need to live like Jesus in every way. He would always tell his disciples, "My time has not yet come." When you have antsy and impatient moments, just remind yourself that your time has not yet come. Trust in God's timing because he knows best.

Instead of worrying about when the blessing will come, spend time studying the Word and being doers of the Word. Don't stand still waiting on God. There is still work to be done for the kingdom. Do your due diligence and make every effort to be found spotless, blameless, and at peace with him" (2 Peter 3:14). And while you do that, God will work in your favor. God will renew your strength, and you will not grow weary.

God came through for Abraham even when he was 100 years old. He also came through for Hannah. And there are many other examples that testify to God's glory. Have the faith of a mustard seed, and nothing will be impossible for you.

Walk by the Spirit

"Therefore, brothers and sisters, we have an obligation, but it is not to the flesh, to live according to it" (Romans 8:12).

"For those who are led by the spirit of God are the children of God" (v. 14). Whatever you want to do, you cannot do. We are to do the will of God. We die to our flesh every day. It is an ongoing process. We don't just get saved, and then that's it. The work started the moment you confessed that Jesus Christ is Lord.

The enemy hates that you walked away from him. So, in knowing this, each day, we must remain strong in faith and prayer. Clothe yourself with the Word and put on the full armor. Even though we live by the spirit, we are still clothed in fleshly bodies. To be absent from the body is to be present with the Lord. "Not only so, but we ourselves, who have the first fruits of the spirit, groan inwardly as we wait eagerly for our adoption to sonship, the redemption of our bodies" (v. 23). While we're on this earth, "count yourselves dead to sin but alive to God in Christ Jesus" (Romans 6:11). "I do not understand what I do. For what I want to do I do not do, but what I hate to do. And if I do what I do not want to do, I agree that the law is good" (Romans 7:15-16).

There is not one of us who is good. As it is written: "There is no one righteous, not even one" (Romans 3:10). There is a sinful nature within us we must resist if we want to be children of God. "For if you live according to the flesh, you will die; but if by the Spirit you put to death the misdeeds of the body, you will live" (Romans 8:13). We must display fruits of the Spirit. The flesh and the Spirit conflict with each other. "Put to death therefore whatever belongs to your earthly nature" (Colossians 3:5). Set your mind on heavenly things, not earthly things. Stay focused so you don't fall into temptation. Let the peace of Christ rule in your hearts.

Wisdom

"Those who trust in themselves are fools, but those who walk in wisdom are kept safe" **(Proverbs 28:26)**

Wisdom is not leaning on your own understanding but praying and trusting God. It is also helpful to acquire wise counsel from an older individual who has increased knowledge, experience, and a strong relationship with God. Job 12:12 says, "Is not wisdom found among the aged? Does not long life bring understanding?"

Wisdom is knowing when to take appropriate action when danger arises and always preparing for the worst scenario. Do not put your trust in man. Be cordial with everyone, but assume everyone has a negative agenda until they prove otherwise. Keep your feet from evil. Wisdom is more precious than rubies and gold. Wisdom can prolong a person's life. Life is not without obstacles, but those who heed wisdom from the Lord find favor with the Lord. Those who obey his instruction will have a rich inheritance in the end.

Every day, there is an opportunity to gain wisdom and knowledge. Wisdom is being not just a reader of the Word but a doer of the Word. Reading is useless if what is read is not being applied. "My son, do not forget my teaching, but keep my commandments in your heart, for they will prolong your life many years and bring you prosperity" (Proverbs 3:1-2). Many people see God's Word as rules, but God loves us and gives us free will. His Word is a guide for how we should live on Earth. If we live according to his Word, life can be very fulfilling. Things won't be as difficult because we have the strength only God can give. That's not to say we won't have our crosses to bear and life won't be difficult, but with the aid of God, we have comfort in his instruction. His commands benefit us greatly and will lengthen our short years here on earth. His commands are not to hurt us but to help us live life abundantly. The fear of God is the beginning of wisdom.

Witnessing

"He said to them, 'Go into all the world and preach the gospel to all creation'" (Mark 16:15).

As children of God, we are not just to be content with our own salvation. We are called to be fishers of men. With every opportunity we receive, we plant a seed, which is the Word of God. Therefore, studying to show thyself approved is so important. How can one advance the gospel if they do not have the knowledge?

Before witnessing, a child of God must have done their due diligence with studying and, most importantly, truly walking with God. If they are not walking with God, they won't be empowered by the Holy Spirit. "But when he, the Spirit of truth, comes, he will guide you into all the truth" (John 16:13). If a person is not walking with the Spirit and tries to witness, the person they are witnessing to could expose them and possibly throw their bad fruit in their face. You can't speak the Word if you are not truly living by the Word. You need to be an example to the world. You are supposed to be the light bearer in a world full of darkness.

God wants us to be prepared to always have an answer for the hope we have. When witnessing, one should first let the person talk first so you can assess who you are dealing with. Other than those walking with God, there are only a few major categories people fit into: the backslider, the lukewarm, and the unbeliever. Once you know what category they fit into, you will know what Scripture to apply to their situation.

For example, if they are lukewarm, then you can inform them of Revelation 3:15-17, which discusses how God views lukewarm people and how he will spit them out of his mouth. When witnessing, do it all with love and respect. Exhibit the fruit of the Spirit, so it may be received favorably.

If you are conversing with the backslider, then you could discuss the parable about the prodigal son. God is like the father in the parable. He will accept the lost child who wants to come back to him.

For the unbeliever, certain general questions need to be asked of them. Ask them if they know who God is. How they respond will let you know how to proceed next. If they are seemingly curious to know more about God and are overall receptive, then you can continue witnessing. If they get defensive or angry, then it's time to dust your sandals off and move on. Some seeds fall on stony ground.

Other general statements that can be used for nonbelievers are these: "nobody has come back from the dead to let us know there isn't a God. If you die and find out there is no God, then you have lost absolutely nothing. If you live your entire life as if there was no God and then you die and find out there was one, you have gambled away an eternity of paradise. Is your soul worth gambling?"

It is also helpful to give a testimony about your own life to not only give glory to God for his deliverance, but to let them know God is able to handle anything. Many people think they have gone too far and there is no hope for them. But you must let them know that if they have breath in their body, it is not too late. They still have time to repent with a sincere heart, take up their cross, and walk with God.

One of my favorite Biblical examples of God's mercy is in Luke 23:39-43. The thief on the cross next to Jesus rebuked the other criminal: "Don't you fear God?" The criminal stated how they were being punished justly but Jesus was innocent. Then he says, "Jesus, remember me when you come into your kingdom." The thief had faith in Jesus and the kingdom of God. The best part is when Jesus tells him, "Truly I tell you, today you will be with me in paradise." What an amazing display of grace and mercy! It is never too late. If the thief had a repentant heart while on the cross dying, then surely, we are given the same chance.

Finally, if you are witnessing to someone close to you, you can get a bit more personal with them because you have the intimate details of their life. You've already developed trust in the relationship. One must always pray that the seeds they plant will fall on good soil. "But the seed on good soil stands for those with a noble and good heart, who hear the word, retain it, and by persevering produce a crop" (Luke 8:15). If the seed falls on rocky ground, then it is not your fault. You've already done your part by planting the seed. The rest is up to them. "Now I rejoice in what I am suffering for you, and I fill up in my flesh what is still lacking in regard to Christ's afflictions for the sake of his body, which is the church" (Colossians 1:24).

Jesus died for us all. We can't let his death be in vain by being selfish with the gospel. Before we accepted Christ, one of his children witnessed to us. So, now that you are saved, you must pay it forward. We must testify to others of our faith. Put others first. This is God's will for us, to witness to the lost sheep, the backsliders, and the unbelievers. With the power of Christ working in you, you can do amazing things for the kingdom. We are to teach, pray, worship, testify, give, and encourage God's people. Only what you do for Christ will last. It is important they understand how sin came into the world, the blood sacrifice, the need for one sacrifice for all, and how to be saved. "For God so loved the world that he gave his only begotten son, so that whoever believes in him shall not perish, but have everlasting life" (John 3:16). Being saved means taking up your cross, being persecuted for Christ, and letting the old self die so you can become a new creature. Walking with God means you surrender to his will. You no longer do what you want to do; you obey God and all his commands.

Worrying

The year 2020 was a year full of worries. How will the children go to school during a pandemic? What do we do about the unemployment rate? There were many uncertainties, but we can always count on God. Luke 12:22-26 discusses how Jesus told the disciples not to worry about life, clothes, and food. He said life is more than worrying about these petty things. He compares us to birds. Birds don't need a house or outfits, yet God still feeds them. How much more important are we to God than the birds? We cannot add a single hour to our lives by worrying about menial things; we are wasting the short time we have on this earth. The harvest is what's important. The harvest is plentiful, but the workers are few (Matthew 9:37). We need to have faith that God will take care of our needs. Without faith, it is impossible to please God.

Isaiah 41:10 tells us not to fear or be dismayed for God is our Lord. He will strengthen and help us. "I will uphold you with my righteous right hand." God comforts us by letting us know we have no reason to be afraid because he will give us strength. He is God. He is always faithful and trustworthy. Isn't it heartwarming to know God is always there to uplift us with his hand? "Have I not commanded you? Be strong and courageous. Do not be afraid; do not be discouraged, for the LORD your God will be with you wherever you go" (Joshua 1:9).

God has given us his Word to abide by. We can be confident in our strength and courage because God is on our side. In everything we go through, God is always with us. He will never forsake us. We take comfort in this, and it soothes our worries in tough times. Cast your cares onto him because he cares for you. He will never let the righteous be shaken (Psalms 55:22). God is letting us know he can always be trusted to sustain us. If we surrender to him and give it all to him, he won't forsake us; He will keep us every single time.

"Trust in the Lord with all your heart and lean not on your own understanding; In all your ways submit to him, and he will make your paths straight" (Proverbs 3:6). We must surrender it all to the Father and submit our will to his. Trusting in him means you don't have all the answers, but you have the faith God will work it out. Don't be anxious about anything but in everything, with prayer and thanksgiving, present your request to God. God will show you the way. He is your Father, and he wants you to prosper.

Stop worrying about what's going on in your life and the world. Put it in God's hands. He will put you in perfect peace. "Now may the Lord of peace himself give you peace at all times and in every way. The Lord be with all of you" (2 Thessalonians 3:16). Jesus is the Lord of peace. He can give you peace of mind in any situation. No matter how big it is, God is able. Take comfort in this.

You Are Not Your Own

"Do you not know that your bodies are temples of the Holy Spirit, who is in you, whom you have received from God? You are not your own" (1 Corinthians 6:19).

When we eat gluttonously or behave sinfully with our bodies, for example, we are sinning against God. Because the Spirit lives in us and our temples belong to God, any offense we commit is also against him who lives within us. We must be careful to conduct ourselves in a way pleasing and acceptable to the Lord. We must represent Christ with our every action.

As humans bound with flesh, we are powerless to fight demons on our own. We need God's help to fight this daily war with our flesh. "May God himself, the God of peace, sanctify you through and through. May your whole spirit, soul, and body be kept blameless at the coming of our Lord Jesus Christ" (1 Thessalonians 5:23). We must let the Holy Spirit guide us in our spiritual walk. We walk by the Spirit, not the flesh. The Spirit will help us control the tongue, the lust, wrath, any vengeful spirit, and so on.

Surrender your whole being to him with a sincere heart. Stand firm until the end, so that you may reap an eternal reward. Let your mind, body, and soul be found innocent when Jesus returns. Your love for God must outweigh your desire to do what you want to do. We are naturally rebellious in our human nature. Let your flesh die daily. Take it one day at a time. Let God fight your battles. Meditate on the Word of God and his promises.

Your Identity in Christ

"So God created mankind in his own image, in the image of God he created them; male and female he created them" (Genesis 1:27).

God is not human, but our spirit was made in his image. We were made to worship and praise the Father. We were given dominion over all creatures. "The Spirit himself testifies with our spirit that we are God's children" (Romans 8:16). We should know our identity when it comes to the Father. We are co-heirs with Christ. We might not have been crucified, but as true children of God, we will endure sufferings for Christ but will also share in his glory. If Christ is in you and you are in Christ, you are a new creature. The old you is dead. You left the old vomit. You are doing a new thing! Don't let the enemy try to question your position. You are a child of God made in his image. With God's help, you can trample over snakes and work miracles. You are a holy vessel made for his purposes to display his glory. Remind yourself of this daily.

"May God himself, the God of peace, sanctify you through and through" (1 Thessalonians 5:23). God's will for you is to follow his commands, worship him, and fight the good fight. As a child of God, you have all the tools you need in this life (his Word). We are called to be peaceful and thankful for what the Father has done for us.

www.ingramcontent.com/pod-product-compliance
Lightning Source LLC
Chambersburg PA
CBHW031532120626
46545CB00005B/2114